NATASHA

Angel Messages

A 333-PAGE
ORACLE GUIDE BOOK

I dedicate this book to my two beautiful children for when I've gone:

To Rishi and Sienna, my blessings in disguise

When times are tough and you feel rough and you feel like you're not enough, Mum is here with you. And if you ever feel scared, alone, lost or confused this is my guidance to you...

The very essence of me is a part of this book. My love and heart is within each word. As you read it, feel the love and absorb it.

Hold this book close to your heart and feel my presence. Then flip the pages for a message of Guidance and Empowerment from your Mum who is now part of the 11:11 Angel team above

x

About the Book

11:11 Angel Messages is a 333 page oracle guide book that has been specially designed to help guide and empower you on your journey. These messages have been fused with channelings from the angelic realm, Natasha Nanda's own experiences and life lessons from Earth Angels physically walking on this plane. These energies combined bring you messages from your 11:11 Team of Angels.

This book will not just aid you on your journey, but others in the collective too.

33.3% of all profits from this book will be distributed to various charities, causes and helping others on their mission to shift the collective consciousness and make a difference in the world.

For more information about the author, charities and causes please visit:

Natasha-Nanda.com or IKeepSeeing1111.com

How to Work with the *11:11 Angel Messages* Oracle Guide Book

This book can be used whenever you need guidance and empowerment from your team of 11:11 Angels. It works like conventional oracle cards but rather than shuffling, you are flipping the pages!

There are 111 messages in the book, each of which have been repeated three times. This is the Power of the Divine Source of 3, giving a total of 333 messages. The chance of you receiving the same message more than once is of no coincidence. It is synchronicity! Your Angels are trying to get your attention, so now is the time to focus on the messages you receive.

Practise using the book and find a method that feels right for you. You can choose one page at random for a daily reading, or up to three pages for a more detailed insight.

How you can use this book:

1. Hold the book in your hands

2. Close your eyes and visualise a ball of white light around you

3. Feel the energy of the book and connect with it

4. When you are ready and your mind is clear, ask your Angels to give you a message of guidance

5. Flick through the pages and stop when you feel called to

6. Choose the left page or right

7. Open your eyes and read your message of guidance

8. Thank your Angels for the message you have received

Or

Look at the *Message of Guidance Contents Page* and choose a title you feel drawn to

Message of Guidance

Contents Page

Abundance

We want you to focus on what you have, rather than on what you do not have. Everything you need, you have access to! The wealth of abundance you obtain from within is priceless and extraordinarily limitless!

We know that the situation you have been facing comes from a deep-rooted perception of wealth that has been embedded within you, from a combination of other people, past lives and conditioning. We want to reassure you that money is not to be feared, nor is it the route of all evil! The fear of not having enough money is really an embedded fear that you are not enough. We want you to know that you are enough, and you are all that you need! When you begin to accept this, you will start to detangle and cut the cords of ancestral ties that bind you.

Remember, there is more to life than materialistic possessions.

It is better to be broke with a beautiful heart than rich with intentions that do not serve you! Do what sets your soul on fire by living in the present moment of 'Now' and you will attract all the love and abundance into your life that you require.

Take time each day to express what you are grateful for; from the love that you receive from others, to the air that you breathe that keeps you alive. When you practise this daily, abundance will shift in your favour!

Acceptance

We can see that there is a great need for accepting what has happened in the past and releasing everything that is weighing down on your precious wings! Know that nobody's life is *'perfect'*. What you perceive in others as the *'perfect'* life may not be the case behind closed doors! We say this with a wink…
"Never judge a book by its cover."

When you accept that you are perfect just the way you are and that you will always have challenges, you will slowly be able to release the load that is pulling you down.

Learn to recognise that every situation aids your growth. When you do, you will surely flourish! When you place expectations on yourself, relationships or work, you limit the progress of your growth.

Remember that:

'Good people' bring you the gift of love, happiness and memories. Who you consider to be *'bad people'*, bring you the gift of experiences and lessons. Both facets can aid your growth. Every person that crosses your path is therefore a blessing and sometimes in disguise!

Accept everything for the positivity that it can bring and you will lead a positive and abundant life. This is because you will be able to accept things for what they are rather than for what you *think* they should be!

Actions

Your soul craves to joyfully serve humanity, but you need to be in an ocean of serenity and bliss to be able to swim and reach your destination.

The secret to success is when you put your mind, body, heart and soul into what you do with love and passion.

It is your love and passion that really fuels your actions in the right direction, which will bring about the change that is needed. To change and move forward, you must start with acting on your own needs first!

Once you have invested in yourself, think about your individual goals and reflect upon what needs to be done to acquire them. Put your energy and focus wholeheartedly into what it is you want to achieve.

Know that your actions mould you into who you want to become, but your words only say who you want to be! Remember that your actions speak louder than your words.

Plant the seeds you want and then plan on undertaking what it is you want to accomplish. Keep those thoughts aligned with only positive thoughts to yield more abundance.

Adjustments

If you are feeling like there is a block to the stream of abundance, finances, or the love that you receive, then you need to reflect upon your current situation and adjust accordingly.

If the problems are within your relationships, family or work life, then change needs to occur from within. Accept that you cannot change other people, but know you *can* alter what you are currently doing.

Most of the stress that you face can arise from the way you or others respond. You can choose to respond by walking away, saying nothing or adjusting your attitude and that additional stress will gradually disperse. It can also prevent unnecessary confrontations from occurring.

When you feel like you do not like the direction you are going in, adjust your sails and redirect. When you master the habit of adjustment, you will see that it is better to bend a little than to break a solid foundation or loving relationship. If things get rough, have faith in us to guide and coast you through the storm until you get to still waters.

Adjustment is not easy, but see this situation as an adventure where all the obstacles you face are mere challenges. It is like climbing up a mountain; it takes time, hard work and perseverance, but when you get to the top, you will be able to reward yourself for your achievements!

Adventure

We want you to step out of your comfort zone and be spontaneous because this is the best kind of adventure your soul needs! The best moments happen when they are unplanned, random and spontaneous.

If you are too busy working or trying to fit in with the rest of society, how will you ever know how amazing you could be or the amazing things you could do or experience? If you are constantly surrounded by people absorbing your energy and you are feeling depleted, go take yourself on an adventure. Happiness, love and adventure are all within your reach!

We can hear your inner child screaming out to be released and we want to see you slow down. Do not worry or rush things, instead honour your inner child by losing yourself in life's simple pleasures!

Now is the perfect time to loosen up and shake that rigidity and routine away. When you begin to loosen up, you will notice other people around you loosen up too. Sometimes the most productive thing you can do is relax.

Life is a beautiful adventure! Surround yourself with beautiful people, things or places. Live your best life and live every moment of it because you only get one chance to do it!

Assertiveness

This reading serves as a reminder to be more assertive when you need to be. Know that it is okay to say *"no"* sometimes. Why say yes to things at the cost of your own happiness?

It is time to concentrate on yourself, to do what needs to be done to move forward and reach your intended destination. You need to focus on thinking about your own needs more and not putting other people's needs first. Having the courage to be honest and open with other people and yourself is essential for your progression.

Getting caught up worrying about other people's opinions or beliefs will not always benefit your progression. Be aware of external factors that may affect any decisions that you make. Allowing or absorbing what others dictate to you will not serve you in the long-term.

Instead, rely on your own expertise and knowledge and apply what you know or feel to the situation, instead of asking for someone else's opinion.

Talk to yourself sometimes, when you need expert advice!

Authentic Self

We want you to find the courage to be authentic. To do this you need to release yourself from everything society and culture has imposed on your beautiful being!

Authenticity is a daily practice of letting go of who you have been conditioned to *think* you are and embracing who you *really* are.

Know that what makes you vulnerable is not a weakness, it is what makes you beautiful, raw and true. Own that vulnerable side that society often labels as a *"weakness"* because we want you to know that it is not! It shows great courage and promotes and facilitates other people to do the same too! As you step into your authentic self, you become a beacon of light to others, helping them feel safe to embrace their true selves.

You are a treasure chest that holds many hidden gems and you are amongst the rarest! When you are living from your authentic self, know that not everyone may like you, but you are growing and transitioning on your path as you should. Be yourself, accept yourself, forgive yourself and value yourself.

When you are in alignment with your true authentic self, abundance and happiness will surge within your remit. You can then bathe in a stream of peace, love and serenity!

Balance

Although the road you travel upon may be difficult, unpleasant, challenging or testing, trust that you can overcome those feelings. Aim to balance your thoughts and feelings to maintain stability and equilibrium. For every bad thought or feeling, cancel it out with a good thought.

Know that your body is a temple, so keep it filled with love and good thoughts. This is a healthy habitat for your soul to live and flourish in. What benefits your soul benefits your life! The more you care for it, the more blessings and abundance you will receive.

Balance is about two things: h*olding on* versus l*etting go.*

Hold onto memories and experiences that lift your soul and make you smile.

If something is no longer positively affecting your life, would it benefit you to let it go? If you do not let go of what is not serving you, will you be able to receive what you truly deserve? With the knowledge that everything you need is on the other side of fear, would you jump?

Taking that leap of faith could benefit you, but only if you balance your thoughts enough to tip the scale and have the confidence to jump!

Balancing Relationships

We have been watching you and see that there is a deep need for you to balance your desires, goals and dreams with the relationships you have with others.

The labour of work, or what you are currently doing at present, requires a balance of commitment with your relationships with your loved ones. This is the driving force that enables you to succeed in any environment. Love is the pivotal force that catapults you to your destination! If what you are doing is burning you out, spend more time doing things that light you up! This will propel you further in the long-term.

Perhaps consider whether you are committed and working to the best of your ability in what you are doing and in your relationships with others. Are you being present in your relationships or are you too busy working, over-thinking or being consumed by technology?

If you become less distracted by things that are not beneficial to your soul, you will generate more time to invest in the things that you love the most. When you become more present, love, happiness and abundance will certainly arise.

Believe

We would like to see you letting go of anything that is currently worrying you by releasing your feelings to us. Move away from the worry of *'when'* or *'how'* things are going to happen. Instead, start changing your thoughts and believing that they will!

If you believe that you can do it or have it, believe that you deserve it and believe that you'll receive it, you will reach abundance and success in all that you desire.

Having belief will give you the balance you require to move forward diligently. Have faith and believe in yourself, and you will be unstoppable!

Reminding yourself and saying these affirmations daily may be the medicine you need to give you the confidence boost required:

I AM Amazing
I AM Independent
I AM Worthy
I AM Successful

Know your worth, then add tax!

Believe in Yourself

This message of guidance comes to you because this is an ideal time for you to think about what YOU want, as opposed to what others *'want'* or *'expect'* from you.

You are the captain of your own ship and you can steer it in any direction you wish to sail! Why allow insecurity or fear to prohibit you from cruising out of your comfort zone and travelling into the unknown? We want you to know that this is where your adventure begins. Yes, it is on the other side of fear!

It is fear of the unknown that can often keep you earth bound. You have the choice to allow your soul to grow and soar beyond the limits of restrictive thoughts and feelings.

Believe in yourself and your talents, knowing that there are no limits except the limits you place on yourself.

Have faith in what you do, but above all, have faith in yourself. There is something inside of you that is much greater than any obstacle or challenge. Rise above your deep-rooted fears and ride on the wings of faith and trust. And remember, you are never alone, because we are the wings that you ride on!

Change

Change is on the horizon and it is to be embraced! Know that this change will benefit you in the long term, even if it feels like an uphill battle.

If you feel like you are struggling, we will send you a direct message of 555 or 5555 on your path. This is a reminder from us that this change is here to benefit your soul! Keep the faith!

We want you to be open to change, starting with yourself. Change occurs in stages within the mind. When you alter your thoughts, it adds more depth at each phase. The result will be the beautiful transformation of yourself and all that you desire from what you have created in your mind.

Know that you cannot change other people, but you can change your behaviour, attitude and actions. If you want a different result, try making a different choice for change to occur. Regardless of what happens, your choice will always serve to benefit you in the long run.

Sometimes your life needs to be turned upside down, shaken and changed to relocate you to the exact place you need to be. Everything happens for a reason. Trust the process; we have got your back!

Change in Direction

We have watched you push yourself either mentally, emotionally or physically. We want you to stop, think and reflect on specific areas in your life that are causing you stress or disharmony.

Take time to focus and reflect on what you have been doing and see where adjustments can be made to help construct the change that is required to reach your destination, even if that means a change of destination. This does not make you a failure; it is about what makes you happy!

If you have a passion, creative idea or project, now is the time to start or finish it. The seeds that you plant with love, hard-work and dedication will bloom and produce a fruitful life for you.

If you want different or better results, think about making different choices! A change in direction could be just what you need to restore the balance in your life.

Change Your Thoughts

Your life is a mere reflection of what you think. If you change your thoughts, you change your life. Work to balance the union of your mind with faith.

The joy that can enter your life is limitless. Joy, love, happiness and abundance is dependent upon the quality of your thoughts.

The more grateful you are for what you have, the better you will feel and the quicker your manifestations will appear.

Balance your thoughts with positivity and then tip the scales so your mindset is elevated above the negative events and people that infiltrate your life.

Let positivity dominate and take the central stage in your mind. It is time to serve an eviction notice to the negative committee that resides in your mind and get positive tenants to thrive inside! A happy mind is a happy home!

Comfort

Even though you have walked through the darkest moments, we have always been present on your journey. We always embrace you with extra love and light to comfort you in such moments.

You may or may not have felt us but know that you have never been alone. We have been watching over you and we are proud of how far you have come, but we want you to be gentle on yourself.

Do not push yourself too much or kick yourself when you think you have made a *'mistake'*. That is how you grow and evolve. Know that it is okay to have bad days, or days when you want to scream and shout. If the only thing you have done all day is breathe, that is enough. Out of the suffering, hardships and traumas, we have seen your beautiful soul emerge and rise, time and time again. The warrior spirit within you can withstand any storm!

When your words fail you or you do not know what to say, know that silence carries the thoughts and prayers to your loved ones in your life and those who have transitioned. Your heart and soul will soon find comfort and peace. Have patience and trust in us. We send you an abundance of love and light to heal your heart.

We place an angelic kiss on your forehead. Feel the love, absorb it and use it to help you get through the next chapter of your journey. You are not alone!

Compassion

We want you to know that every small act of kindness goes a long way. You are here to make an impact in the world but remember sometimes less is more!

Working hard and earning money is not the only way to success. Do not underestimate the power of a hug, smile, a kind word or compliment; a shoulder for someone to cry on or a listening ear. They can have the potential to turn someone's whole life around.

Compassion not only helps others rise but it also helps you too. If you want to be happy and turn your life around, try practising compassion with yourself too! Here is our extra nudge of guidance to you:

Consider reducing the food, people or environments that deplete your energy and leave you feeling tired, frustrated, or low.

Add some fun, adventure and happiness into your life as part of your daily routine.

Relax and rejuvenate your mind and body by disconnecting with technology for at least half an hour before going to bed.

Engage with us and connect with mother nature by getting some fresh air and re-connecting back to source.

Have compassion for yourself, by taking **CARE** of you!

Completion

You chose this page because we need to give you a gentle nudge in the right direction!

We are here to remind you to take the steps and actions required to continue moving forward or completing intended goals. Habit, persistence and perseverance is what will see you through to the end.

If you have an idea, start to implement it now, envisioning it in completeness. If you have already started something, continue to execute it to the finish line. Do not expect others to do it for you - the ball is in your court now! It takes focus, determination and practise to aim high in order to succeed.

Achievement, success, desire and dreams are all connected with action. Even if you feel like you will or are making *'mistakes'*, keep moving and do not give up. You can do anything if you shift your mind into positive gear! When you do, you will be cruising in the fast lane in no time!

The best thing you can invest in is YOU! Have faith and courage in your own abilities and see things through to the end.

Confidence

We have watched you successfully overcome so much and we commend you for this!

We believe in you, but we want you to have confidence and belief in yourself too because that is when the magic starts to happen. You will then grow and transition into a beautiful butterfly!

Know that confidence is not about being better than others, it is about having belief in yourself and not comparing yourself to others.

You are a strong individual and we want to reassure you that you have the courage to speak out and do what it is you want. Confidence thrives from leading from your true authentic self and being honest with what you know, say and do.

Declutter what does not serve you so you feel lighter and can move with grace and ease. The most beautiful thing you can wear is a smile! Think of your smile as your armour of confidence even in the bleakest of days and it will help you march on.

You are a beautiful energy of love and light and the world needs to feel your presence. You were born to shine!

Contemplation

If you feel like you have come to a standstill in a specific area of your life or are currently stalling, contemplate on what could be holding you back.

Reflect upon your past and present circumstances and unearth any potential knowledge or expertise that will help you move forward. Remind yourself of the love that is or was once around you. Feel and breathe in the memories and harness that love to move you forward in your situation.

The road you are on may sometimes feel uncertain, but at least you are on a road. You just need to decide which direction you want to go. Trust your intuition for it guides you well.

We want you to know that to achieve anything externally, you must first contemplate changing how you think and feel internally. If you change your focus and let go of what does not serve your highest good, you create space for fulfilment to enter your life. The road ahead then becomes much clearer.

Start each day with gratitude and love. In return you will be blessed with all that you need. When you operate like a magnet, you will attract everything that matches your frequency. Now that is something serious to contemplate on!

Courage

We are here to give you the strength and courage you need so you do not resist the changes that are unravelling in your life. These changes are here to help you evolve and grow, not to create a feeling of being stuck or paralysed. Gather and receive the strength that we send you and stand tall to whatever comes your way.

Have the courage to make the changes you need and the strength to see them through. You can do this! You are strong! Even though it may feel like everything around you could be falling apart, perhaps it is really falling into place. We see this and in time you will too.

It takes great strength to stand alone! We admire and love this quality you possess. Your individuality brings you the gift of freedom and flight. It takes great courage to become who you are, and for this you will be rewarded with great abundance.

Remember to maintain the connection with yourself by staying in the present moment of now. Remain balanced, grounded and aware so that you have the clarity to summon the power of strength and courage that dwells within your beautiful soul.

You have a warrior spirit. Do not allow your past to define you.

Your past does not define your destiny!

Cultivation

We want you to know that your body and mind needs to be cultivated in order to work effectively and efficiently. What you feed your body is just as important as what you feed your mind.

Fertilising your mind with kindness and love, and your body with healthy habits and substances, are vital! When they are both functioning in unison, this will produce a reservoir of energy.

If you have something to start or complete, now is the time to address it. Everything that you have been contemplating, planning or doing will start to come together when action is taken. Your hard work will inevitably pay off and you will start to reap the rewards, but you must have the energy contained within for you to release the energy needed to harvest your intended outcome.

The journey from the start of conception to completion may be challenging but enjoy and embrace every moment by remaining present. Having the determination and patience, whilst learning from the challenges you may face will be an asset to usher you along the way.

Take the necessary steps to start or complete what you set out to do by cultivating what you wish to grow. It is then that you will be rewarded with fruits from the seeds that you have planted!

Declutter

If you feel like your life is full of chaos and disharmony, this is a sign that you need to declutter!

Clutter is not just the things in your wardrobe or in the environment around you, it is anything that gets between you and the life that you want to be living. This includes the clutter that resides within your mind too!

Start decluttering your mind and the environment around you. If it does not nourish your soul, get rid of it. It is the unnecessary things that you hold onto that have the aptitude to stunt your growth. If your possessions or thoughts that you hold onto are not serving you, it will not be serving you any better in a box collecting dust or locked up in your mind. Releasing what does not serve you helps your mind and body heal on many levels.

Making space in both your environment and mind allows new opportunities, relationships and ideas to enter your field. When you release the baggage that holds you down, you feel lighter and begin to soar to new heights!

The *"Out with the old and in with the new"* motto springs to our mind! Perhaps you can use this as your affirmation to aid your task of decluttering!

Direction

We feel that there is a deep need for you to contemplate the route you want to travel along, letting your heart navigate you.

We want you to recognise that direction is more important than the speed you are travelling at. You hold the key to your vehicle in your heart and mind, but first you must have faith and trust in the route you envision. If you can see it, feel it and believe it, the path ahead will become much clearer.

At points on your journey you will need to rely on your own intuition and independence. If travelling alone makes you feel fearful or anxious, know that the journey you face unaccompanied can also make you the strongest! Remember, walking alone is sometimes better than walking with people who do not value you!

Remember, you are in control of the steering wheel. You decide which direction you want to go in!

Have faith that the journey you are on is destined for you and has a purpose, however tough it may seem. Know that there are no bad decisions, as there are always lessons to be learnt from every situation. Keep moving, one foot in front of the other. Small steps are better than no steps!

Disconnect To Reconnect

We want you to be mindful of your current environment. Know that you can walk away from anything that does not serve you or make you happy. This does not always mean just physically walking away, but mentally and emotionally too.

Declutter and disconnect from any negative words or actions, being mindful not to respond, react or retaliate. In these situations, silence is the best remedy. Do not be the one that fuels the fire, as the only person who will get burnt is you. Hold your integrity this is everything!

Have faith that any struggles you are facing at present will soon resolve. Spending time by yourself, reconnecting with mother nature, crystals or listening to meditation music will help you zone out from everything that distracts you. This will also help re-energise you and give you the nudge you need.

To hear yourself and our guidance, you need to be able to disconnect to reconnect again. This can only be done if you unplug the undesirable thoughts and people that pollute your mind! When you feel more grounded you can re-plug yourself into the world because you have rebooted your system to full optimism!

Divine Connection

You opened this page because we want you to know that everything you need is available to you when you connect with us. We want to get our messages through to you, but we cannot do this when you are not paying attention.

Communication is a two-way process and we want to talk to you! Take time to pray and meditate so that you can hear and feel our loving presence, support and guidance. We send you signs and synchronicities daily, but you need to slow down or stop to notice them!

Try to separate yourself from technology and the pressures and worries of life, in order to reconnect with us. Ensure that you reconnect with yourself too, by maintaining your needs and filling yourself up with self-love and care.

When you do this, you become more in-tune and in alignment with your being and soul's guidance. Only then will we be able to guide you at a much deeper level than we already are. Trust in us as we trust in you!

When you are connected to us, you become attuned to the solutions that you are seeking. This divine connection is a special avenue that will bring you transformation faster than you can imagine!

Divine Guidance

Our divine light surrounds you with a shield of love and protection. Call upon us for support and guidance to give you the strength and courage you need to put your armour on and overcome any struggles you face.

We want to help you! We have noticed that you have not been grounding yourself enough. Ensuring that you are grounding helps to keep your roots firmly planted on the ground. Strive to spend more time outdoors, allowing the oxygen to revitalize your soul. This will aid your body into adjusting to what is potentially destabilising your alignment. This will assist you in weathering any storm you may face.

Remember who you are and the faculties that you possess. Everything you need to overcome any testing times are stored inside you! Just sprinkle a little faith over the situation and this will aid you in moving forward.

We are your safety net; here to soften the blow and catch you if you fall. Take comfort in the knowledge of this. Trust the process and find the strength, confidence and courage to elevate your soul above the toxicities of life. Above all, keep the faith your story does not end here!

Dreams

We want you to know that your dreams are important. So why put other people's dreams above your own? We want you to know that you matter! Anything is possible and everything is within reach if you have faith and believe in yourself.

Spending time focusing on things that do not serve you such as fear or judgements, will inevitably push your dreams further away from you. Creating a plan and then implementing it is a beneficial tool to help execute your dreams into your reality. Why allow your fears to erase or alter those dreams? The choice is yours!

Spend more time doing things or connecting with people that bring joy into your life. This will elevate you to new horizons. You have an abundance of love within you waiting to be unleashed, but only you can lower those barricades for it to fully shine and bask in it's ambience!

Pay attention to signs and messages that we send you. If you see peacocks, know that we are watching your progress and are proud of how strong and far you have come.

The impossible can come true. Do not let anyone stop you, but most importantly, do not be your own obstacle in reaching your dreams! You are an important part of the jigsaw, do not lose your place to anything or anyone! Make a move, there is no time like the present!

Ending of a Situation

You received this message because we want you to know that the ending of a situation and a beginning of a new one is near.

Remember that the relationships around you play an important part in your journey and all serve a purpose. Know that people come and go in your life like the seasons that constantly change. This can bring both pain and joy, but know that it will help both you and them in your growth and progression.

Be aware that it can be difficult to start the next chapter and end any situation you are in if you keep re-reading the last one. Release what is not serving you with love and light, so you can finish what was started, be that in work or a relationship.

Protect your energy and do not allow any negativity or drama to lower your vibration. Instead, turn this negative energy into fuel to succeed in any projects, ideas or work that you are currently undertaking. This is how you can turn pain into power!

When you make any decisions, have faith in the choices you make. Execute this with assertiveness, not allowing other people to doubt your choice. You know what benefits you. Trust your own authority and intuition for it will guide you well.

Energy

We have noticed that your mind and body have been in constant over-drive. We suggest creating time to relax, take a break or slow down.

Take time to meditate or connect to our divine energy. You have the power to access it whenever you want and to gain a deeper insight. Tap into this energy as it will guide you on your journey.

Life is for enjoying and when you enjoy what you are doing, your energy naturally amplifies. You will then be vibrating on a higher frequency and become much more proficient in what you do.

The energy you emit creates your life. If you are feeling drained or tired, your energy is not functioning as well as it could be. Take some time to stop and recharge in order to heal your soul and receive the optimal energy for you to perform.

Keep your vibrations elevated by ensuring you are looking after your wellbeing. Fill yourself up with self-love, care and worth. This is a necessity for your journey!

High vibrational energy is infectious and has the aptitude to spread ripples far and wide. For what you deliver, you also receive!

Energy & Vibration

You can create abundance with the power of your mind but be aware when your mind is acting like a yo-yo and your thoughts are up and down. This is a sign that you need to stop!

Allowing negative thoughts to dominate your mind will only attract negativity back towards you. Allowing anxiety, doubt, fear and worry to distract you, will lower your vibrations! Instead, focus your energy in being with people who you love and make you feel happy and content. Maintain this state of mind and you will open a gateway for abundance to flow through.

Put your time and energy into setting your intentions with belief and hope. Visualise what it is that you want. Feel it, believe it and imagine receiving it. The positive vibrations of energy that you emit, you will attract!

Once your mind is released from the prison of your thoughts, you will be more open to obtain what you desire because you are vibrating at a higher frequency. Your thoughts and words are a vibration of energy. You must learn to change them so you are vibrating on a harmonious frequency to support what it is you want to receive.

Remember, the raw capability of the mind is limitless!

Faith

We surround and comfort you with a blanket of love and strength. Hold onto it tight and feel secure in the presence of our unconditional love. Faith is invisible, but it has the power to connect you to what you need.

Allow your faith and love to be bigger and stronger than your fears. Fear is an energy that contracts and love is an energy that expands. Envision a bright, white light encompassing your being whenever you feel deflated or like you want to give up. Love is light and this is what will help you expand!

Your faith can shift any obstacles but be mindful that your fears can also generate them. Let go of anything that weighs you down and do not doubt yourself! If doubt creeps in, inhale confidence and exhale fear.

You can change the scene of your life at any time from the energy around you. Spend time reconnecting with us and nature, drawing these harmonious energies into your soul.

Know that faith resides within your heart and it will give you the strength you need to take that next step. Have faith in yourself and trust that you have the power to overcome and do anything! If you see 222 or 2222, that is a direct message of guidance from us to remind you to *"Keep the Faith!"*

Faith in Yourself

See your current situation as a challenge and not as an obstacle. Trust in us and know that a positive outcome is being brought to you. It will align in your favour when the time is right. For now, continue moving forward with faith and remain patient and optimistic.

Know that faith can move mountains but remember, your doubts can create them. If you have lost someone dear to you, know that their presence in your life has given you the tools for you to move forward in difficult times. Reflect upon these and use them to help aid you at this crossroad. Only you can shift the course of your journey through the passage of your actions!

We encourage you to have faith in yourself. Do not ever give up because of one bad chapter in your life. Keep going and do not lose hope. Know that your story does not stop here. Miracles happen just before you are ready to quit!

Be mindful not to compare yourself to others. Learn to feel genuinely happy and content with who you are. Only you can decide who you want to be or what you want to do with the power of your mind and the faith you have in yourself.

We want you to know that you are amazing and you are good enough! Believe in yourself, as we believe in you!

Family

We want you to know that families are like branches on a tree; they grow in different directions but their roots remain as one. Even when you lose people you love, they always remain within your roots. Whenever you miss them, spend time outdoors near a tree to help you reconnect with them and yourself.

Ensure that you are doing what makes you happy, rather than striving to serve and do things for others. This will only burn you out and lower your vibration because you are not in alignment with your true authentic self.

Taking care of yourself is extremely important, as it contributes to your ability in taking care of others. You are the root of your family but you need to be grounded for it to flourish. Remember that family is not always defined by blood, sometimes it's defined by love.

Spend time grounding and connecting to nature and doing what helps you grow. If that means temporarily disengaging, then go with the flow and let it be.

You are your own unique self and you have your own unique branch. Know that it is ok to outgrow what you once were doing and change direction. This is your life so do not be afraid to live it your way and reach the heights that you dream of!

Fill Yourself Up!

Love is the most powerful energy that you need right now. If you are not receiving it, this can deplete your energy. You do not necessarily need to look to others for love but you can look towards yourself and fill yourself with self-care and love instead! You can always rely on your own branches to keep you elevated!

Take time out to do something you enjoy, be that with friends, family or going to a special place on your own. When you fill yourself up with love and give it to yourself, you will be able to pour with the excess love you have preserved!

Be assertive and remember that it is okay to say no to others. You cannot receive what you have not given to yourself. Give yourself love and it will be given back to you. Self-love and care are crucial when you feel depleted!

Shed what no longer serves you, releasing any fears, worries and problems. If you do, you will be fuelled to gravitate towards love, abundance and success.

When you do what you love, your soul becomes content. This is the environment you need to be in to flourish!

Fresh Air

If you feel down, lost or demotivated, take time out to disconnect and recharge your batteries. Open some windows, go for a walk and let the abundance of fresh air revitalize you.

Your mind, body, spirit and soul need some fresh air to heal, rejuvenate and ground your beautiful being! Spend time absorbing yourself in and around nature.

Connect with everything around you; smell, see, feel and hear the beauty in nature that surrounds you. Breathe it into your soul and feel the increase in energy levels. This will open your mind and offer you a fresh perspective.

Spending time in nature is an abundant source of healing that costs you nothing but your time. Investing your time in nature will raise your vibration and is the greatest force for your wellbeing.

You can also switch off from the disturbances of life, toxic situations and people by spending time enjoying your own company. This will give fresh air to your mind because you are silencing the disruptive noise in your head. Sometimes when you disconnect, you reconnect with a stronger signal!

Focus

Have faith in our capability to lead you to abundance. All that you need is available to you, but you must learn to focus your mind and express your intentions clearly to us.

Spending time focusing on your own individual needs is imperative on your journey. Where focus goes, energy flows! Ensure that you are pouring all the love and energy into yourself first.

Starve your distractions and feed your focus by using mindfulness techniques and incorporating them into your daily life. A clear mind helps you to directly focus on the road ahead.

Practise inhaling abundance into your life and exhaling all negative thoughts and feelings. Only then will the areas of love, work and relationships begin to prosper.

Give gratitude to everything in your life and your circuit will flow in a synchronistic and harmonious state.

Stay focused on whatever you want to do, not allowing self-doubt to hold your mind and heart captive! Whenever you find yourself doubting how far you can go, just remember how far you have come!

Gratitude

We want you to know that the life you are currently living is like a mirror. It reflects your thoughts, feelings and actions.

Get into a habit of having uplifting thoughts in the morning and before you go to bed. This can change your whole day.

Ingraining daily gratitude into your thoughts each day is important to raise your energy and vibration. The more gratitude you give, the more things you will receive to be grateful for!

Focus on seeing the light at the end of a tunnel when times are a little low or rocky. When you acknowledge all the things that you already have in your life, these acknowledgements will build the foundation for the abundance that you will receive. The more gratitude you express, the stronger that foundation becomes!

Gratitude is a tool that can be used to maintain your physical, mental and spiritual wellbeing. It is the best medicine, for it heals your mind, body and soul. Expressing gratitude, either verbally or written down, is your vitamin for the soul!

Gratitude is like a boomerang; what you throw out into the universe will always come back to you in some shape or form!

Growth

You have grown so much on this journey and we are proud of all you have done and achieved. Think of all the things you have achieved and what you are grateful for because these have contributed to your journey and where you are now.

You have an inert ability to shine your light but remember to make sure you protect your light so that you are not depleted. You cannot give to others if you do not have enough light to walk your own path.

You are the torch of divine love and light and we intend for you to share it with others, but do not give away your health in the process! It is okay to say, *"this isn't serving me"* and walk away in peace. You have the power to do this because you are a strong individual!

Remember that growth can be painful and lonely but like the caterpillar in the cocoon, with time and patience, you will break out of where you are residing and transform much stronger and more beautifully than before.

We would love to see you disengage from technology and reconnect with us and yourself. This is where you will grow in reflection.

Grounding

We know that you want to feel free and fly high in everything you do but we want you to know that in order to fly, you must start from the ground. The more grounded you are, the higher you will fly.

It is through practise, patience and perseverance that you will begin to navigate through any storms you may face on your path. If you are feeling all over the place, use some of these grounding techniques to help you:

-Walk barefooted, connecting with mother nature.
-Hug a tree or meditate underneath one.
-Visualise yourself either under a tree connecting to the roots or even better, be the tree!
-Wade in water, fill your lungs with fresh air by going for a walk or opening your windows.

Raise your face to the warmth of the sun and connect with the fire. Raise your face to the bright, shining moon and connect with the light. It is then that you will feel and absorb the vast power and energy within your very being!

Nature does not just ground you, it also nourishes, heals and transforms you. It helps you to grow and blossom into the beautiful being you were designed to be!

Happiness

Finding time for the things that light you up and make you feel happy to be alive is where you need to be! You deserve to be happy and to live a life you are excited about. Do not let others make you forget that.

Anywhere or anything that ignites happy memories and brings an abundance of joy to your soul is the environment you can safely bathe in. We want you to find your happy place and we feel that it is important that you make this your number one priority right now!

Everything you need to help, heal, rejuvenate or motivate you, resides within you internally. There is no need to look externally for it.

Living in the past and observing others can prevent you from reaching happiness. Instead, be in the present moment of now and look within to find the happiness that will navigate you towards your dreams!

Be happy with what you have. Gratitude alone can bring happiness to you because what you give out, you attract, so always be grateful!

Healing

Your health is of great importance to us and we want you to function in its full capacity. We love and care about you but we need you to do the same too!

Commit to yourself by maintaining your physical, emotional, psychological and spiritual needs. Eat foods that nourish your body and indulge in healthy habits.

Be present and surround yourself in high vibrational environments such as listening to uplifting, empowering music or affirming strong, inspiring, daily mantras to elevate your emotional and psychological state of mind.

Heal in the presence of nature; listen to uplifting or serene music, soak in a salt bath, exercise, treat yourself, practice daily gratitude, read self-help books, practice mindfulness, meditation, prayer, yoga and Pilates.

If you feel like you are overthinking and struggling to tame your thoughts, try taking time to practise any of the above. This will enable space for enriching things to attract to you. When you are at peace with yourself, happiness will follow and this will aid the healing process.

Honesty

Honesty is a highly valued and positive quality to possess. Do not expect it but appreciate it when it is freely given.

In relationships, honesty is valued and appreciated and it is where trust is gained. Respect and loyalty can then be given in return. Being honest may not get you many friends, but it will always get you the right ones. It is quality, not quantity that matters!

The power of honesty can be unearthed when you decondition what society has infiltrated in your mind. Do not pretend to be someone you are not in order to impress others or conform to certain expectations.

You should always strive to be your most genuine and authentic self. If you want to experience freedom and happiness, do not hide anything. The greatest advantage of speaking from your authentic self, is that it will flow with ease and you do not have to remember what you said!

Be who you are, not what you think other people want you to be because you will only be travelling your journey as a lie.

Be true to yourself, integrity is everything!

Independence

This page serves as a reminder for you to take a break to reflect and regain the strength for you to independently move forward in the current situation you are in.

Know that you are not alone and your loved ones you miss are always present within your beautiful heart. Remember that after every storm, a rainbow follows. When you see a rainbow, know that this is a sign from a loved one giving you a message; to have courage and to remind you of your strength!

We urge you to spend time with yourself. Solitude is a place where your mind increases in strength and learns to lean upon itself. Your mind then becomes self-sufficient and you no longer need to rely on the advice or opinions of others. When you look within, all the answers will surface. This will guide you to your destination and bring happiness into your life.

You have the power to construct the life that you want. Do not be afraid to speak up for yourself or say 'no' when you do not want to do something. You are much more powerful than you think. Now, trust your power and believe in yourself. It is your independence that will give you the wings to fly!

Individuality

We want you to know that you are a precious gift to the world and here for a great purpose. You are a unique individual and that is your superpower!

You are enough and there is no need for you to imitate or copy what others are doing. Whether you realise it yet or not, you are here in this world to be an original, not a copy! Remember to be led by your true authentic self because this is what makes you stand in your superpower of individuality.

You are a beacon of light and can reach people in dark places. If you ever feel like you are in a dark place or feel vulnerable, fill yourself up with self-love and care. Most importantly, be kind to yourself.

Know that your vulnerability is a beautiful attribute because you are having the courage to be seen for the authentic individual you are. Vulnerability is your greatest measure of courage. Remember that courage does not mean you do not get scared, it means you do not allow fear to stop you!

Step outside of your comfort zone and the box that society has put you in, regain your power and shine your own beautiful light. Be the unique individual you were designed to be!

Infinite Love

We want you to know that infinite abundance is available to you. One of the most significant forms of abundance is love.

If you put pressure or expectations on your relationship with yourself or others, this will only deter you from your path!

We want you to be aware that it is possible to create your own heartache by having expectations of others. Remember that love has no expectations. If you do not expect anything in return, you can never be disappointed!

Rely on your wings and the self-love you pour into yourself to give you the independence you need to stand strong. When you embed this into your mind on a daily basis, you will release the conditioning of the expectations put on love. You will become free to enjoy the things for what they are, instead of what society has made you think!

Love is infinite but loving yourself is the greatest revolution! When love has no expectations, rules or limits, love thrives. Remember to apply this wisdom in your life.

You are an infinite being who has the capability to access infinite abundance. Use the power of love to create a life you love.

Love is energy and energy is contagious. You always gain when you give love!

Inner Child

It is time to awaken and reconnect with your inner child again. This is where your true authentic self resides. It is the original piece of you that is pure, innocent and connected to your heart. Honour your inner child by living in the present moment of now. When you lose yourself in simple pleasures, you recognise how much there is to love about life.

This is how young children live and they are the most precious gifts in the world. It is now time to unleash your inner child as it wants to come out and play!

Spend time in the company of young children and observe their world through their eyes. Ask questions, get involved and perhaps you will see and feel the magic in everything too!

You may be growing on your journey and in age, but you can still stay young at heart if you unleash your inner child.

Remember when you were young, wild, curious and full of life and energy. Do not let life tame that beautiful authentic side. Embrace your inner child and you will experience a tremendous amount of love and healing. This is needed for your soul to thrive!

111 Intentions

If you see 111, know that we are encouraging you to wake up, pay attention and align yourself to an elevated thought frequency. This page serves as a reminder that you can manifest anything into your reality. If you think about your intentions, feel it and believe it, your thoughts will create all that you wish.

Before you go to bed and upon awakening, you can programme your subconscious mind with what you desire, as if you have already acquired it. A habit of doing this daily will transport this into your reality.

You create your reality by the thoughts and seeds that you plant but you must nourish them daily, watering them with feelings of faith, love and joy. If you focus on what you want, your power of intention will intensify with great speed. Always remember that your thoughts hold significant power!

Intuition

Yes, your soul knows exactly which way you are meant to go, but you need to release what does not serve you in this current situation so your soul can lead you there! Only then can you be guided by your intuition, rather than other people's negativity, opinions, beliefs and expectations.

Silence your mind from distractions so that you can feel our loving presence and hear your intuition that is built within.

Pay attention to our gentle nudges through signs and synchronicities that we send you to know that we are helping you on your journey.

We also want you to be mindful of your emotions. Ensure that they do not override or interfere with any decisions you need to make. Respond when you are in a calm and collective state so you can articulate yourself more coherently. Be guided by your feelings and led by your calm thoughts and doors of opportunities and reconcilements will transpire.

Intuition is like a muscle; to develop it you must listen! When you have developed the ability to listen, allow it to be your internal compass to always guide you in the right direction!

Invest in Yourself

We want to support you in fulfilling your potential. Spending time worrying about who likes or dislikes you will potentially deter you from your purpose. When you invest in your own thoughts, happiness will follow.

Life is a journey of ups and downs but you hold the key to create the life you desire. Happiness, love, success and dreams are all yours for the taking, but you must use the key to unlock those treasures. The key to doing this will be released when you learn to make yourself a priority. Self- love and care are imperative in the journey you embark upon. Self-love is not a selfish act but a necessary one!

Invest in filling yourself up with self-love and care because your life purpose is much greater than you know. You need to be optimising at full capacity to achieve all it is you intend on accomplishing. Listen to the whispers of what your body, heart, mind and soul need and then act upon them.

Invest your time, passion and commitment to your visions and goals and you will soon reap the rewards. The amount of energy you put in is what you will receive, but do not forget the greatest investment to propel forward is in yourself!

Joy

We love you for who you are and we want to see you filled with joy. We need you to accept yourself for the wonderful person you are and not be ashamed of how others see you.

If you are spending too much time attempting to make others happy, you are only sacrificing your own happiness in the process. Remember that you are only able to give to others that which you have yourself.

If you are not happy, self-care and maintenance need attending to. Always take the time to improve yourself before you start improving other people or things.

Remember that it is important to continuously bring joy into your life and to value yourself. When you are centred in joy, you have the power you need to swiftly move forward. If you are feeling trapped, give your worries to us and we will lift you up.

The key to being happy is knowing that you possess the power to choose what to accept and what to release. Let go of anything that does not serve you because it does not deserve you!

Lightworker

You are a lightworker and here for a greater purpose. We are aware that you are at your happiest when you are helping others.

People are drawn to your veracious energy and the light that you radiate. Be aware of your own energy supply and ensure you are not depleting when offering help and advice to those who need it. With your highly attuned empathic abilities, it is quite easy to absorb their emotions or negativity to drain your own energy. It is vital that you learn to ground and protect your auric field!

In order to help make the world a better place and awaken others to the true beauty of life, it is essential to lead the way by example. Listen to your body and soul when you are feeling tired or low, this is a sign that your energy is depleted.

It is necessary to take time to rest and recharge your batteries and close yourself off temporarily for spiritual maintenance. You can only give and serve others if you are in a place where your own cup is overflowing.

Pay attention when you see lights flickering. This is a sign that we are with you and a reminder that you are guided and protected by the light. Your energy is a beautiful and powerful force. You have the power and gifts to raise the collective consciousness and shift humanity to another dimension!

Love

We want you to know that we love you, but we want you to love yourself too! When you feel love for yourself, that love will enable the strength and courage your warrior spirit has to transform pain into power!

Take time for self-care by doing something that you love and enjoy. Be mindful of what you say, think, feel, do and eat. They all require attention and awareness so you can flourish.

If something hurts, let it ricochet off you by responding with love. If you harness your emotions in the direction of love, you become more balanced.

If your thoughts and feelings are taking control of you, ground yourself. Inner peace is required in this situation. To find it, silence your mind from distractions. Do not be in a rush to do or say things.

Let any worries bounce off your energetic field and release yourself from the shackles of fear that burdens you. It is then that you will be able to drop the load that weighs you down, so that you can spread your wings and fly in the direction of what you love.

Love & Commitment

Self-love is an ocean and your heart is a vessel. Commitment into self-care will produce an over pour of love both for yourself and humanity!

This is a divine time to concentrate and put the love and commitment into what sets your soul on fire! The things that bring you joy make you happy, and when you are happy, abundance follows! You can then inject this into your work, relationships, goals or dreams.

Aim to keep your intentions and actions balanced and in unity. Take more time to balance your work, family and social life. When you have balance, everything else will begin to fall into place. If you act with love, you will receive acts of love in return.

Love is patient; quality time needs to be invested in yourself so that you can function better. If you decide to commit to something, make sure you invest the right amount of time and effort to fulfil this. Remember, love and commitment are acts not words.

Stay motivated and continuously remind yourself that YOU have the power to create the life you want, but you must invest in yourself with happiness and love first!

Luck

We bring you good news… Your luck is about to change and abundance is on its way!

Keep your thoughts beating in tune with the rhythm of your heart and the sound of your dreams. However, be mindful that if your thoughts come out of alignment, everything on the outside can change too. Remain positive and open to the doors of opportunities that reveal themselves to you and walk through them with confidence.

Be conscious of how you use and nurture the lucky streak or abundance you receive. Think before you make any rash moves and this will inevitably support you in the long-term.

Recognise that faith, belief and perseverance assist you in acquiring the abundance that you receive. Do not forget to reward yourself for all your hard work too and show gratitude for the positive luck that you have received!

Motivation

A wealth of infinite abundance will be yours if you are motivated enough to attain it. The biggest source of motivation is in your thoughts. Train your mind to keep trying, not allowing thoughts of failure to tie you down.

Fearing failure can essentially cancel out your motivational streak. When you feed fear with more fear, it thrives on this environment to survive. Instead, have no limits and make no excuses, otherwise fear will continue to breed. You can do anything if you completely immerse your mind, body, heart and soul into it, with passion and love!

If you get knocked down, what motivates you to get back up?

Whatever this is, you can use it to push yourself every day because no one else is going to do it for you. This does not mean you need to overexert yourself. Small steps are okay too, there is no rush.

Spend time reflecting and planning what you need to do first and this will help you be more efficient and will save you time in the long run. The time and dedication you pour into what you are doing or intend to do, will produce an overpour of abundance.

So put your motivation pants on and get moving!

Moving others

We have seen that you have an inert ability to move people with either your presence, words or touch. You have a magnetic energy that attracts people into your field. Your power to inspire and empower others is moving, motivational and inspiring!

This ability you have to help others also creates a positive energy around you and sends ripples far and wide. You do not always see or hear about how you have impacted others, but we watch and see the beautiful ripples you have created. We want you to stop for a moment and acknowledge all that you are and all that you have done! For this we honour your soul and thank you!

It fills our hearts with joy to know that you can show people how to embrace what they perceive to be '*flaws*' or '*weaknesses*'. Know that the guidance you provide to other people helps them more than you realise, so continue to do what you are doing.

If new people cross your path or old people appear in your life, know that it is for a great purpose. Keep moving with the rhythm of your soul and it will guide you to where it yearns to go. There you will find satisfaction, joy, peace and love.

Move with Love

Love is the driver that steers you towards your destination. You cannot move without it. It will benefit you if you let go of any resentment or anger you hold onto, because it will only prevent you from moving forward diligently.

If you feel like your emotions are taking control of you, spend time meditating or praying, clearing your mind from distractions so you can receive the guidance you need.

Make a conscious effort to spend more time with those you love and be grateful for what you have and how you received it. In order to build on your relationships, commitment is required by investing time and love into them. But first you need to pour love into yourself. This is not essential, it is necessary!

The source of your actions should always come from a place of love. Work hard on giving love daily to yourself then to those around you and the work you do.

Spend time doing something that satisfies your soul. Time invested in self-care and love will rejuvenate and re-energise you, so that you can focus on the outcome you want to receive.

Music

If you are feeling low or you are struggling to focus, listen to high frequency sounds or music to help stimulate you and heighten your energy to vibrate on a higher level.

Remember that music and sounds can rapidly affect your mood and alter your vibrational frequency. Listen to music that makes you feel empowered, inspired, motivated and uplifted. Singing also helps you feel the vibrations more powerfully within your body.

Music has the power to change your world and the world of others around you, if you learn to feel rather than just hear.

If you are struggling to sleep at night, try and meditate with calm, relaxing music to ease your mind and soothe you to sleep. Through music, meditation and sleep, your body will be able to heal and recover from any stresses that have been troubling you.

Remember that we always send you signs and messages in the music that you listen to or hear around you. Pay attention!

New Beginnings

We want you to remain patient. You are soon to be offered a new beginning, opportunity or fresh start.

No matter how old you are, you are still capable of starting new ventures and trying new experiences. Remember that sometimes some things must come to an end for a new doorway of opportunity to open. Let go of anything that no longer serves you or adds any benefit to your life and embrace what is to come.

You will experience new feelings and emotions when you begin this new chapter in your life. It may take time to adapt to, but embrace this new change with patience and trust!

We will send people to support and guide you through this transition, so be aware and mindful of the wisdom that they bring you. Wisdom is a beautiful thing as you can draw upon different aspects of other people's lives. This is a beautiful gift!

Have faith in your dreams and do not let anyone infiltrate their negativity into your field of happiness. Embrace and accept your own individuality and strengths. This is your time to shine and be who you want to be!

New Project

We want you to know that this is your life to live the way you want. You are in control of your own destiny!

If there is a new project you want to start or continue and you are feeling blocked or demotivated, take a step back to reflect. Consider what you feel is preventing you from growing and what you need to do to move forward. If it helps, write this down on a piece of paper so that you can see a clear structure on how to start or progress.

Focus on the end goal you wish to actualise and hold this clearly in your mind. Let go of any worries or concerns about how you are going to get there and trust that everything will work out.

No matter what your current circumstance is, if you are able to imagine something that sparks a light within your soul, you will be able to create something better for yourself.

Embrace your individuality within this new project and you will succeed in anything you do. There is no one else in the world like you and that is your unique power! Do not follow other people's footprints or path. Instead, create your own.

Notice the Signs

We want you to slow down so that you can notice the signs we send you. Look out for number sequences, feathers, dimes, robins, hummingbirds, rainbows and ladybirds. These are all signs you are on the right track and that you are being guided by us and any loved ones who have passed away.

We also want you to be aware of what other people are going through. Remember, you notice more when you are silent and observing. Think before you speak or react. This is our wisdom to you.

If you notice any signs of pain, negativity or anger in others, tap into your compassionate nature to help them but make sure you do not absorb their feelings or energy. As an empathic soul, it is crucial that you protect your energy by firmly grounding yourself.

You can also help those who are suffering through prayer, intention or meditation by sending them love and light. This will also help you with your own healing and growth as well as theirs. When you are serving others through the eyes of love and compassion, you receive that love and healing back to yourself as well.

Open Your Heart

It is okay to open your heart and let people close to you. Do not allow any previous experiences of pain and suffering become an obstacle in your current relationships.

When you expect love and you are let down, your soul can feel crushed! Fear, anxiety, confusion, pain and disappointment can overwhelm you but If you master the mentality to have no expectations, you will never be disappointed! Finding a place of joy will assist in extinguishing the pain and hurt that you have previously experienced. But to do this, you must first step out of the walls that imprison your heart.

Know that your soul does not always need protecting from love. If you learn to love yourself, you will have all that you need and that will be enough to let your guard down. Always remember that love does not necessarily have to come from others.

Be grateful for everything and everyone already around you and what you possess. But most importantly, look for love within. It is only when you learn to genuinely love yourself and embrace the individual you are that you can put the energy into loving everything and everyone else.

Opportunities

In order to make space for new opportunities, it's essential to abandon what does not aid you in your transformation. Everything you think, feel and believe, you attract into your energetical field. We want you to be aware of your thoughts and actions because every action has an equal reaction.

Focus upon what it is that you want, but do not worry about how or when this will come to you. Believe that you have the power to manifest anything you want, and we will orchestrate the opportunities for you.

Have trust and faith that we are working in your favour to help you fulfil what it is that you need and desire. Pay attention to the signs that we send you, you may not notice them if your mind is working in overdrive!

By practising gratitude daily, you will draw everything you need like a magnet. This is when doors of opportunities will present themselves to you unexpectedly. Remember that the power of the mind is the key to your success. Gratitude is the vitamin for your soul and the vital component to opening the doors of abundance and opportunities into your life.

Trust the process and remain patient there is a plan in place for your beautiful Soul!

Organisation

We want you to invest in your time wisely. Organisation will help in shortening the road to your goals and dreams and reduce stress and clutter in the process. This will save you time and money, thus giving you a better quality of life and more freedom to grow and move in different directions.

Remember that organising or cleaning is a practise. Stay on top of it, being mindful not to get complacent because this will only deplete your time and energy further down the line. Being organised requires discipline; if you practice this every day it will become a habit that will aid you in your everyday life.

When you organise your environment and mind, you release all the clutter that does not serve you. This disarray, chaos and imbalance affects your energy and can block you from moving forward on the path of abundance and opportunities.

Organisation enables you to manage and take control of your life and have clarity in all that you see and do. Remember that a tidy space is a tidy mind!

Overcoming Challenges

Rather than looking at problems as obstacles, see them as challenges that you can overcome. Unfortunately, being challenged in life is inevitable, but succumbing to it is optional. You have the choice to bulldoze through any challenges that you meet.

We understand that life can often feel difficult with these challenges that you face but have faith that you will reap the rewards if you continue to persevere and overcome your trials and tribulations.

Know that you have the strength that is needed to overcome every hurdle and adversity that you face. When you challenge yourself, you will realise the true potential of who you can become or what you can do!

Visualise yourself as a tree, keeping your roots grounded and you will be able to weather any storm. Remember that after every storm follows a rainbow!

Stand strong and have courage as your companion to guide your way. Keep the faith and know that the situation you are in will soon subside. We are working behind the scenes to help you. Trust in us as we trust in you!

Patience

We can see your frustration in a specific area of your life and we want you to know we are supporting you. Trust in us and have patience.

Patience is not about the ability to wait, but the attitude you have whilst waiting! Build a relationship by communicating daily to your inner and outer needs and take the time to nurture them. You do not necessarily need a mind that is speaking, but a patient heart that is listening. It is then that the insight and support you require will be presented to you.

Learn to accept that things can happen in different ways, rather than the ways that you expect. Everything happens for a divine reason and everything is coming together as it should to benefit you in the best way possible.

Have faith that opportunities and abundance will soon be presented to you. Do not allow your faith to waiver. Worry and fear ends where faith begins. Remain patient and know that everything comes in divine timing. Trust in us.

The best things in life are worth waiting for!

1111 Pay Attention

We are your Angelic team and you were drawn to this page because we are nudging you in order to get your attention. Pay attention to the signs, synchronicities and people that we bestow upon you on your journey are rare treasures in disguise. Do not allow your judgements to intervene, as this would be unfavourable to our intended outcome for you.

When you see 11:11 or 1111, this is us reminding you to stop for a moment and become more aware of your surroundings, thoughts and feelings. Look around and observe everything that you can see, hear, feel or sense. These messages we send can be embedded within songs, numbers, repeated words or advertisements that you see or hear.

Sometimes the things that you believe to be minor, are more important than you think. When you really pay attention, you will see that everything around you is guiding you!

Perseverance

No matter how hard the road ahead may seem, you must keep moving forward. Remember that forward is forward, however slow you go!

We are cheering you on, so keep pushing yourself in the direction of your purpose and soul calling! Believe in yourself and push through the limits that you or others place in your way. Tough situations build strong people!

Do not give up, even when you feel like you want to. The world loves a stubborn heart. If you fall or make mistakes, it is okay, you can still get back up! We believe in you.

Never think that you are a failure. You only fail when you stop trying! We are ushering, nudging and shaking you to move forward and keep going! You can do this!

If things are really draining your energy, take a break to relax and re-energise and then get back on the path you were walking. You may not have reached your destination just yet, but you are closer than you were yesterday.

Remember to be kind to yourself and do not be disheartened. It is often the last key in the bunch that opens the door to where you want to enter!

Play

We have been observing you and we want you to know that more time needs to be made for having fun!

We have noticed your mind and body have been working hard lately and your energy levels could do with a boost! Too much work and not enough play is not good for the mind, body or soul.

You cannot give your energy to other people or projects if you do not have enough reserved for yourself. Therefore, it is essential to take time out for yourself and participate in activities that satisfy your soul and help re-energise your being.

When you spend time in a state of "play", you can release the load that burdens your precious being. Spend time being with or around children and release your inner child that is yearning to be set free!

See, feel and listen to the world from the goodness of your heart. Smile, laugh and bask in the ambience of fun! This will open your senses and give you more clarity and direction in your life.

This is what your body requires to restore your energy. When your energy is restored, you become more effective and efficient in everything that you do.

Positive Thinking

We want you to know that in order to change your situation or receive what it is you desire, it is imperative that you keep your thoughts saturated in love and gratitude.

If you alter or connect your thoughts to a frequency of positivity, this will align you physically, mentally, emotionally and spiritually. It is then that you will be open to attract an abundance of all that you wish for and desire.

Seek to understand that your thoughts and choice in words have the power to help change your actions and environment around you. Rather than fearing *'what could go wrong'*, instead ask yourself, *'what could go right'*? Yes, you have the power to flip the script at any time!

Go for a walk and spend some time in nature so you can disconnect from everyone and everything around you! Silence your mind and all that distracts you and then try to look at everything from a fresh, positive perspective.

Sometimes all your mind needs is a bit of tender loving care and training! Tame the negative committee in your mind and you will have 20/20 vision to see the path you were born to follow.

Practice

In order to rise to the challenges that you face, you must be prepared to change and break the habit of self-limiting thoughts, feelings and beliefs.

You build your own reality with your thoughts. Your reality does not create you! However, if you do not practise using your thoughts wisely, it can mould you into someone you are not.

Motivation is what gets you started, and habit is what keeps you going! If you want to change your life, it is important for you to change something daily. The secret to success and growth is in your daily routine.

Get into the habit of practising doing the same thing each day, so you are always moving one step closer towards your goal. Practising gratitude, mindfulness or meditation, will help ground you in breaking those negative thought patterns that can debilitate you. The more you practise and focus on investing in a healthy environment for your mind, the greater the abundance you will receive. Your mind will be less cluttered with thoughts and feelings that do not serve you.

The power of the mind, combined with action, will combust into an explosion of abundance!

Progression

We are here to remind you that you are strong! Stay positive because every step brings you one step closer to your goals! No matter how slow you feel like you are going, remember that you are moving. Every step counts!

Know that it is okay to stop, take a break and do *'nothing'*, but if you get back up you are progressing! A little progress each day adds up to big results. Love the *'work in progress'* that is you!

If you feel like you are drifting, ground yourself and clear your mind so that your heart can communicate to you. Go for a walk, open some windows and allow the fresh air to rejuvenate your mind, body and soul. A clear mind leads to a merry heart!

When change occurs, do not resist it. Resisting change is resisting your growth and we want to see you progress and grow on your journey! You cannot become or do what you want if you remain where you are. See any challenges as an opportunity to progress and grow to a heightened state of wellbeing.

Your life does not improve by chance, it improves by change! Change can be difficult and chaotic, but in the end it will be beautiful and inspiring to yourself and others. Keep on going, you have got this!

Protection

Have courage to stand firm and hold your space in order
to protect your energy field. Be aware that holding onto
pride, resentment or anger can potentially prevent you from
expanding. Holding onto these qualities is like holding onto a
hot piece of coal with the intention of throwing it at someone
else, but the only person who will get burnt is you!

In order to prevent you from absorbing negativity, getting hurt
or lowering your energy and vibration, release anything that
does not serve you.

Shield and protect yourself by visualising a pure white
bubble of love and light around you, especially when in toxic
environments or when you are feeling depleted. We are always
here to protect you and give you an extra shield of protection
when you call upon us in this way!

Know that love can penetrate the field of negativity and
darkness in your life, but remember that darkness CANNOT
penetrate love and light!

You are a Warrior of Light and here for a divine purpose! Have
faith that you can withstand any storm. Visualise yourself with
an armour of love placed upon you, so you are ready to enter
any situation that you may face with courage and valour!

Purpose

Know that everyone discovers their soul purpose at different stages of their lives and this is orchestrated divinely! If you know your soul purpose, do not lose sight of it. Know that every 'bad' day serves a purpose and aids you in your progression.

If you do not know or fully understand your soul purpose yet, do not worry. Everything will unfold as and when it should. Everything happens when it is intended; trust the process and keep moving forwards.

Know that your path is not always a straight line sometimes there are twists and turns along the way. If you go down the *'wrong'* road and you get *'lost'*, do not worry. You may think you are lost, but you could be exactly where you need to be and perhaps about to discover something significant to aid you on your journey in the future. Remember, everything happens for a reason!

The experiences you have endured so far have taught you valuable lessons to help you grow. Your strength arises from the continuous efforts and struggles that you have overcome. We have watched and supported you throughout these times and we are proud of your achievements.

Realign

We want you to know that grounding is essential right now! The energy within your body is like a wheel that is spinning and rotating. We can see that you currently have blockages within this energetic wheel, and we want to help you realign them.

Make sure you are grounding daily by connecting with nature, meditating, holding grounding stones or crystals. Seek out energetical healers to aid the restoration process. Even healers need healing!

Do not lose sight of your purpose by allowing your negative experiences from the past or present pull you down. This will only interfere with your vibration and energetic field.

Know that any challenges you face are happening for a purpose and when you accept this, you will start to grow.

We want you to know that you are a lightworker here to help others learn and grow from your own experiences. That is why you are a warrior of light! You can help them overcome the fears they face and show them a different perspective. However, before you do this, you need to have the energy and capacity within yourself to act upon this.

You have a significant influence on the destinies of many others and it is therefore vital that you are perfectly aligned.

Reassurance

We can help you restore anything you need and change it into something amazing. All you need is faith in us and yourself! Do not let one *'bad'* day or situation make you feel like you are enduring a bad life.

We walk beside you and hold you up in your time of need. We are gently guiding you on your path, but you need to work with us to help you heal or move forward. Have trust and faith that we will answer your calls.

We surround you with love and light, giving you gentle nudges through signs and synchronicities. Be open to receiving these by paying attention and being more aware of who and what surrounds you.

If you see feathers, know that we are offering you comfort and reassurance and know that you are not alone! This is also a sign that your loved ones who have transitioned are also with you, giving their support to you during this time.

We envelope you with a warm loving hug and embrace you tightly. Feel this love and use it to help you get back up!

Recharge

You were guided to this page because you need to recharge your beautiful soul!

We want you to understand that your life is all about balance. We have noticed that your body and mind have been working in overload and it is time to recharge and restore your energy. We need you to relax, have some respite and take care of yourself.

What you may think is doing *'nothing'*, is actually what brings everything you need into perspective. So, by doing *'nothing'*, you are in fact doing quite a lot! You are resting and recharging. Go with the flow of it opposed to fighting it, otherwise you will burn out fast! You may not see this right now, but we want you to know that this is what is needed!

The question we want to ask you is...

"Do you recharge yourself as much as you recharge your phone?"

Invest in recharging yourself so that you have the power to keep going and moving forward every day.

Pamper yourself with love and attention so that you can prosper. The key to recharging is in self-love and care, which resides in your habits and disciplines. When you wake up every morning, look in the mirror and compliment your radiant being. Recite affirmations to empower the inner Jedi that is screaming to be released!

Relationships

We want you to allow faith to be the driving force to receive abundance in your work or relationships. Let go of any financial or relationship worries that you currently hold. Have faith that we will see you through this situation.

Know that we are diligently watching you throughout this process. The stronger your faith, the stronger the relationship becomes and the stronger you magnetise what you want into your life.

Know that good relationships do not just happen overnight; they take time, commitment, perseverance, love and patience. Build upon these daily with those around you and life will become more balanced.

We want you to know that you are never alone, even at times when you feel like you are. If your heart needs companionship, seek friendship and guidance in us and other people who love you like friends or family, but most importantly yourself!

We love you and want to give you the love you require. Commit to what matters the most but know that you are a priority. For relationships to manifest or prosper, you need to maintain your own needs first.

Relationship Cycles

We have noticed that you have been in the presence of people that are toxic, unsupportive or discouraging. We reach out to you to break out of these repetitive cycles. If you have done so already, we salute you for your courage, for we know how difficult it can be to detach from those you love or care for.

Understand that change occurs for a reason, as will the circle of friendships and relationships you are in. Allowing the fear to enter your space can delay or obstruct the changes and growth that is required for you to move forward.

We want you to know that we are here to lighten the load of what weighs you down by giving you the strength you need to rise above it. Change has a much grander purpose, which will serve you in the future.

Call upon us when fear creeps in. Equip yourself with your armour of courage and stand tall with conviction! You have a choice to walk away from any situation that does not feel right.

This is a good time to spend time with people who raise you up, not pull you down!

Release

We have noticed that you have been holding onto things, which are suppressing your true authentic self. You must heal and restore yourself by releasing any fears or emotions that are blocking you. Resisting this process will only deter you from your path. You have the strength to face anything!

You may feel that a lot of issues you face run in your family, but we are here to guide, empower and reassure you that this pattern does not need to continue with you. You can break the ancestral ties that are preventing you from moving forward.

Know that you can transform pain into power and even empower others from your own personal experiences. This includes any trials, tribulations or harrowing events you have faced.

When you choose not to respond to an emotional impulse such as anger, rage or heartache, you are halfway there! Release any emotional energy and focus on acceptance, as this will help restore the balance.

Know that the past can be painful, but the beautiful thing about it is that it forces you to learn what does not serve or benefit you for your present and future journeys.

Reward Yourself

Yes, a big angelic high five from us! You have been working hard in all that you do and we want you to relax, unwind and reward yourself!

Give yourself credit for the good choices you have made or the things that you have been doing, however insignificant or small you may think it is. Remember that every action creates a ripple effect far and wide. We have seen these ripples and we are proud of the positive impact that you have had on those around you.

Know that it is okay to celebrate personal achievements, even if it is just getting out of bed in the morning or going to work when you do not want to. No one else may understand what it took for you to accomplish them but know your worth and reward yourself for anything good you have done.

You deserve to reward yourself and a little extra self-love and care will only fuel you further!

Rise

We can see that you want to soar above to new heights and that your inner self needs to break free from unhealthy habits, relationships or environments that prevent you from rising.

Love is the key that unlocks the shackles that prevent you from flying. To break free, you need an equal exchange of giving and receiving love. When you feel love for yourself, you come alive. This vibration will radiate and be felt by those around you and returned in kind.

Do not worry about your fears, instead dissolve them with love and light. You are a warrior! You can fight any negative or toxic situations and rise stronger than ever before. Nourish your mind, body and soul with positivity, healthy foods and love.

Rise above the bombardments of any challenges you face and, like a phoenix out of the ashes, you will be reborn!

It is time for you to fly to new, wonderful heights and awaken a new state of being. You can do this, but you may need to drop the heavy baggage that is weighing your precious wings down!

Self-Care

If you are depleted, low or emotional, self-care is required before you burn out! This is our warning to you. Listen to your body when you need to rest and rejuvenate. If you do not have energy, you will struggle to carry out the work that needs to be done.

We see that it is time to fuel yourself up by pampering the needs of your body so your mind can relax, and your heart can slow down.

Support yourself by maintaining and nourishing your mind, body, spirit, and soul. It is important to give yourself permission to take a break and enjoy life!

Applying self-care into your life will make you more efficient and productive, creating an opening for change to enter. When you make space for yourself and declutter, you will be able to hold a space to help others too.

You will find that this brings you great pleasure, satisfaction, and fulfilment. This cathartic feeling is both soothing and healing. Remember, life is for making, but do not forget to look after yourself as this is vital for your development and growth!

Self-Love

This message of guidance we give you serves as an important reminder for you to look after yourself more. It is necessary for you to cultivate your growth, by watering yourself with the love that you need.

We need you to know that you are important and that seeing yourself as a priority is essential on the path you walk on, especially for your progression. It is necessary for you to make sure that you are spending enough time on yourself. The love you give to yourself is the love that you will receive back, and your soul thrives on this.

Your body is a vehicle of love and light, but you cannot arrive at your destination if your tank is not filled up! You cannot give to others what you have not got yourself. Fill yourself up with love, joy and peace and your heart will be open to receive.

It is when you wholeheartedly feel the unconditional love for yourself that you can become a beacon of light for others and truly put the energy into loving everything else.

The relationship you have with yourself sets the tone for the relationships around you. Remember that love must start with you first!

Self-Maintenance

It is easy to get wrapped up in the hustle and bustle of life, but it is important that you remember to take the time to stop and care for your mental, spiritual and physical wellbeing.

Make a conscious effort to introduce small habitual changes, focusing on self-maintenance. Give yourself time to relax, rest, take a break or have fun to enable your body to flow in its natural rhythmic state.

Indulge in things that make you feel good and increase your energy. When your mind, body and soul are nurtured, those things that cause you stress or worry are less likely to penetrate your energetic field.

Fill yourself up with self-love and care. Self-maintenance will help you re-energise and aid any healing that is needed.

When you give love and light to yourself, it will come back to you like a boomerang in other areas of your life. Love is the most powerful energy that can propel you forward and heal anything!

Self-Respect

We have seen that small pieces of you have been chipped away by people and circumstances. But it is time to re-inject yourself with confidence and re-empower yourself with self-respect!

Walk away or distance yourself from anyone who makes you feel less than you are worth or drains you of your dignity and self-respect. Remember that your value does *not* decrease based on someone's inability to see your worth!

Always speak from your authentic, loving self. Do not get drawn into any unnecessary dramas. Sometimes, the most powerful thing you can say and do is nothing! Do not allow your loyalty to become slavery. You do not owe anybody anything!

Save your help and guidance for someone who *does* deserve it. Those who value your support and treats you with the love and respect you so dearly deserve.

Your self-respect is sacred and one of your most treasured possessions. Remember who you are, reclaim your power back and learn to recognise when and what to let go of with love and light.

Self-Worth

Self-worth is vital for your wellbeing and happiness. If you do not feel good about yourself, how can you feel good about anything or anyone else?

Know your worth and do not settle for less than you deserve! Why allow people at work or in relationships to treat you inadequately, just because you love them or because of what they have done for you? Remember you do not owe anybody anything!

We want you to know that you do not need to find your self-worth in other people, you can only find it within yourself. It is then that you will be able to attract a job or relationship that is worthy of you! Work on being in love with the person that you see in the mirror, that person who has been through so much and is still standing!

Nobody is entitled to treat you less than your worth. If they do, learn to walk away or distance yourself from them because they will only continue holding you down and suppressing the beautiful being that you are.

Do not allow anyone to dull your beautiful sparkle, you were born to shine!

Service

You will notice that others around you will become more drawn to you to seek your help and guidance. Use your experiences and inner wisdom to help them. The tools you have are all within you, trust in your instincts to guide your words.

Always remember that helping others also helps yourself because you rise when you lift others up, consequently shifting your energy to vibrate on a higher level. When you lose yourself in the service of others, you will discover your own happiness and understand what makes your own light shine brighter.

Be aware of your boundaries and learn to recognise when your energy starts to become too depleted. It is good to help others but make sure you find the right balance. Remember to always look after yourself too.

You cannot give to others if you have not given to yourself first. Feed yourself with an abundance of self-love and care and declutter what does not serve you.

We are a divine source and we are always here to help you, should you need any guidance. Just call upon us and we will always answer your call.

Slow Down

We urge you to think before making any big decisions at this moment in time. It does not benefit you to continue your daily life in a rushed, tired or stressed state, and we therefore need you to take a moment to breathe and slow down.

It is important for you to understand that rushing things can often result in a less qualitative outcome. Slow down, regain your strength and then get back on the road with a patient, calm, clear mind. You will still reach the same goal, but you will feel a lot lighter carrying less stress along the way!

Try and do things that give you a sense of enjoyment and fulfilment and allow any stress or tension that you have been harbouring to gently ease away.

We ask you to be more mindful and aware when you need to give love to your body and mind. Know when enough is enough and when you need to stop! If your body and mind are feeling tired, exhausted or depleted, this is a sign that you need to take a break, relax, refresh and re-energise.

Remember, life is a journey not a race!

Solitude

Sometimes you need to disconnect from the world to be able to reconnect with yourself and gain more strength. There is nothing more refreshing and rejuvenating than your own company!

Spend time in solitude to connect with your inner self and find the happiness that dwells within. Start a daily gratitude journal to help you reflect upon what makes you feel good every day.

Take a step back from matters that distract you and do not serve you or your purpose. Trust your instincts and do not allow others to influence your decisions or knock your confidence. Be guided by the stillness of your mind, as opposed to other people's chaotic minds.

Have patience in the situation you are in. Gravitate away from overthinking, as this is not healthy for your mind or body and can drown out the sound of your inner voice.

Remember that solitude is not just about silence, it is also about the absence of distraction!

Soul Guidance

Your experiences and circumstances are both connected. These things do not define you but mould and prepare you for your journey ahead.

It may feel like you are isolated and alone at times but know that this can help you navigate towards your soul's purpose. Sometimes when you lose friendships or relationships, you find yourself on a different path and it is here that you may discover your passion and purpose.

Block the thoughts of what others think you '*should*' do, otherwise your feelings of what you '*want*' to do become obstructed. Remember, it is your passion that will lead you towards your purpose, not others.

Your soul is your definitive guidance system. It acts as a compass, map and destination, all in one. Listen to your intuition; this is your soul's guidance. It can be heard when the mind is calm and disengaged from the distractions around you.

We want you to know that whenever you feel lost, down or in despair, turn inwards! When you enter the silence of your soul, you can ask for healing and guidance on your path. You are your own passport home!

Strength

We want you to know that you are not alone. If you are feeling lost, do not give up hope. At times you may feel like others do not understand you and that is okay. There is no need for you to explain or justify the decisions you make or the things that you do. Stand firm with conviction in all that you do, having faith, belief and courage in yourself.

Reflect on a difficult moment in your life that you overcame, then use that experience and the lessons you gained from it to encourage and help you in your present circumstances.

Look deep and find the brave warrior that lies within. Do not accept defeat, you have the power, courage and strength to get through this situation that you are in!

Look in the mirror and see yourself with a vision of love and acceptance. Affirm to yourself your strengths, abilities and skills. By doing this, you will hold space to receive more abundance and love into your life.

The light inside you shines brighter than the darkness around you never forget that!

Success

This page is a sign that magnified abundance and success is on its way. All roads that lead to success require self-belief and hard work, but we want you to balance this by taking time out for yourself too.

Know that behind every successful person there have been many challenges, mistakes and failures. Be kind to yourself and know that all of these serve a purpose, even though it may not feel like it at the time.

Be aware of unexpected openings and opportunities that are offered to you. Do not let them pass you by because of fear or anxiety. Dissolve your fears by creating an image of a butterfly in your mind, blow it into your hand and then release your worries or uncertainties by blowing it out with love and light and visualising them fluttering away!

Let your imagination and creativity lead you to the fortune and dreams that you crave. It is then that your hard work and dedication will pay off and you will reap the rewards of the seeds that you have sown.

Support

We feel that you need to take some time out to reflect on a situation that you are currently experiencing or something you have been contemplating.

Be aware of the positive people around you who are genuinely overjoyed by your success and are compassionate and empathetic when you are sad. These are the people who deserve a special place in your heart and who you can comfortably surround yourself with. They are there to uplift you and help guide you on the path that you are on, so listen to their advice and help with an open heart.

Anything is possible when you have the right people there to support you. This does not have to be just family, but friends and even strangers too! Pay attention to those people we send on your path to help guide you.

You are divinely supported in this situation and although you feel isolated at times, you are not alone. Feel our loving presence, comfort and support, which will help you on your journey. Know that you have the strength to push forward, breaking the barriers that confine you.

Synchronicity

You chose this page because we have been trying to get your attention. What you or others may deem a *"coincidence"* is in fact synchronicity. We are orchestrating and weaving a web for you to notice the patterns, signs and messages that stir the soul. This is us communicating to you!

We leave you a list of several ways we try to get through to you:

On your social media timeline and feeds, number sequences, feathers, rainbows, spirals, coins, sparks or animals.

Conversations with others or when reading, watching, listening to the tv, radio, books, magazines, newspapers, advertisements or internet.

In the clouds, epiphanies, visions, road signs.

In the music lyrics you hear or sounds, smells, feelings and senses that resonate or speak to you.

All of these signs above that you see or hear repetitively are prompting you to be aware of your thoughts, feelings and intentions. If you see one of these frequently, how does it make you feel? What does it represent to you? If you don't know, stop and think about it until something resonates!

It is time to wake up and notice the signs and messages we bless you with!

Take a Chance

We send this message for you to consider taking a chance on changing what you are currently doing and to release your inner self from the walls that you have surrounded it with.

Do not allow your soul to be locked away because you fear taking a chance on something. If you allow fear to drive your decisions, you could miss out on all the wonderful things that life has to offer you!

You can overcome those hurdles you fear by rising above them and acting now. If you try but fail, get back up and try again! There are so many opportunities calling out to you, but you need to take a chance and take that leap of faith!

See life as an adventure by having fun and living in the present moment of now. Contemplate doing something new that pushes you beyond what you '*think*' is your sanctuary. Your sanctuary is your state of mind, not your environment! It can be found in places where you are happy and experience a state of bliss! This will help you on your journey.

We want you to create space to play more and work less. Trust your soul's guidance and you will experience greater freedom.

Take Small Steps

There is no need for you to rush into things. Instead, proceed forward with small steps first and take your time in making decisions with a clear, calm mind.

Make a conscious effort to think before you speak. Try to gather your thoughts and feelings first to prevent any explosive situations from occurring.

Relax, release and recharge when you need to. Life is all about progression and growth, but you are also here to experience happiness, satisfaction, and love. There is no need to put unnecessary pressure on yourself to move at a quicker pace.

We want you to know that there is no elevator to success. You must take one step at a time on your journey. Although the staircase may take longer, the rewards will be much more fulfilling at the end!

Progress is impossible without change, so take a chance on doing new things and more opportunities will appear. Remember that slow progress is better than no progress! Work hard but do not forget to play and enjoy yourself too.

Technology

We would like to see you and your loved ones disconnect from, what we perceive to be, the needless desire and addiction of using technology. You need to reconnect with who you are, what you truly require and what you have right in front of you.

We have observed that technology is like a drug, consuming and wasting much time and energy that could be better used elsewhere. When you are out, look around you rather than looking down at your technological device and see what everyone else is doing.

Do you want to be part of this system, or do you want to be free to release yourself from these shackles that confine you and the loved ones around you? The choice is ultimately yours!

Spend less time using technology and more time enjoying and appreciating the people and things around you.

Beyond your phone and laptop there is a beautiful world waiting for you to experience the endless wonders it has to offer. Go out and play!

Time

The time that you have is precious and we often see it being wasted. We want you to take the time to reflect upon this…

Ask yourself who and what you are spending your time on? Think about those who might be depleting your time and energy. Consider whether your time might be better served with those that add value to your life.

Heed our words of loving wisdom…

Time costs nothing, but it is valuable and priceless!
You cannot possess it, but you can benefit from it.
You cannot keep time, but you can spend it.
Once you have lost it, you can never get it back!

If you are chasing money for happiness, why not chase happiness and let money flow to you from doing what you love?

Time is not only measured by the hands on a clock but also by your internal rhythm and a collection of your experiences and memories. The reason we urge you to spend your time more wisely is to ensure you continuously experience life in alignment with what benefits you. This keeps your daily rhythm beating on a happy, content note.

Time Management

We feel that now is the time for some quiet reflection. When you know how to silence what distracts you, it is then that you become more aware of where and how you can better use your time.

Stop saying: '*I don't have time to do things*' or '*there's not enough time in the day*', as you are only creating obstacles for yourself! Consider where you can adjust things to create more time. It is up to you to invest your time into what is important to you. No one else is responsible for this but you.

Write down what you need to do and organise a structured plan of how and when you will do this. You can then effectively manage your own time and expectations, as well as others.

It is important to include time for yourself and your loved ones. When you balance your time with the needs of yourself, you become more focused and ready to face each day.

Transition

If you are going through any changes or disruptions in your health, finances or relationships, rest assured that this situation is only temporary.

It is now time for you to transition into a new area of your life. You need to remain grounded and make yourself adaptable to coping with this change.

Sometimes transition happens when you least expect it so be prepared!

Know that transitioning is a continuous process, which enables you to progress and grow, and start fresh chapters in your book of life.

You will find that, in these transitioning periods, you will shed parts of yourself. You will notice that your circle of friends may change but rest assured that this is all part of the transition and the ebb and flow of life.

It is when you are in a transitional period that you start to come alive, breaking the barriers that once constrained you. From a cocoon that was in a dark place, you then become the beautiful butterfly that is ready to soar to new heights! Remember that change can be good too.

Trust the Journey

You have awakened to the world around you and are beginning to understand the true mechanisms of how it works.

Continue to travel down the road of spiritual awakening and you will start to see and feel the light more than ever. When you trust the process of your journey, you will see everything unfold to ease you on your path.

Know that you can do anything you want and manifest anything you focus on. Relationships, financial and work goals will begin to manifest into form when you balance your spiritual and materialistic lifestyle. Give gratitude daily and soak yourself in self-love to recharge your energies, especially when you feel lost, down or drained. It is imperative to give your body what it needs!

You have overcome so much and because of that, you have the strength and power to get through anything that attempts to knock you down! You are a warrior and are protected by us.

Unison

When you are feeling downhearted or confused, it could be because your heart and mind are not working in harmony. Unity is strength and when the heart and mind work in unison, wonderful things can be achieved. Your body and soul will then gravitate towards love and joy.

In order to form in unison, fill your mind with gratitude and joyful memories that make you laugh or smile. Go for walks and breathe in the fresh air to rejuvenate your weary soul. When you are feeling lost, connecting and spending time in nature will help you find yourself again.

A lot has changed and will continue to change around you, and because of this, so will you! You are ready to come out of the cocoon that you are currently hibernating in so you can transform into a stronger and wiser being.

Cherish and appreciate what you have at present and what you have received. If you have lost something, think about the experiences, lessons and wisdom it brought you. It is when you choose to focus on the good things you have in your life rather than the things you do not have, that you begin to work in unison with your heart, body, mind and soul.

Unleashing Love

Love is the most powerful energy known to mankind and you hold the power to unleash it from within your beautiful being! We want you to know that it is not about changing yourself, it is about loving yourself. You do not need anyone else to complete who you are, you can do that yourself!

If you are in a situation that you have been in before and it is impinging on your heart, change needs to occur for you to progress. Reflect upon your past experiences with what is happening now. Notice the similarities and differences and then consider what you could do differently. If something keeps repeating, perhaps deeper lessons need to be learned to help with your spiritual growth.

Love requires hard work, time, commitment and passion.

If you feel like you have a hole in your heart, the only person that can fill and complete it is you!

We feel the pains contained within your heart as they are ours too. We know that your heart needs love, but the greatest gift you can give yourself is to spend more time on loving yourself! It is then that you can break free of any cycles or patterns that are holding you back. That is the magnificent ripple effect of unleashing self-love and care!

11:11 Wakeup Call

You are in the supreme powerhouse of 1111 and this is our 11:11 wakeup call to you! Yes, if you have not already, it is time to wake up, pay attention and follow your heart's calling.

Your journey to find or lead your true-life purpose is upon you. You opened this page because we are nudging you to wake up and shift to where your heart and dreams yearn to go.

Set your intentions and feed them with positive thoughts. Recognize that your words, thoughts, and feelings contain great power. Utilise them to benefit you by nurturing your mind like a garden, pulling out the weeds that have the capability to take over. Water yourself daily with love and remove what does not serve you. Only then will you grow as the beautiful soul you were designed to be.

You are here for a much grander purpose. You are a warrior of love and light who can aid humanity in so many ways never forget that! When you see 11:11 or 1111 know that you are never alone and that you are guided by us always.

Warrior Spirit

It takes great force to face other people's opinions and criticisms, but you can overcome this. We know that you have done it before and we want you to know that you can do it again! When you can silence other people's voices from your mind, your own voice can prevail!

This is your life and nobody else's, so take the reins and control it by releasing the warrior spirit within you! Be courageous and assertive in any decisions that you make. Rather than thinking about what you cannot do, focus your thoughts and attention on what you can and will do!

You are standing with an army of Angels beside you, you can do anything! There is no need to lower your expectations to fit in. You are perfect just as you are! We want you to know that you were born to shine, so never let anyone dim your beautiful sparkle.

Everything you need is already inside you! That is the secret people do not tell you. When you feel like giving up, we are the voice of hope that whispers, *"try again!"*

Your warrior spirit will always succeed because you were born with it!

Wellbeing

We are worried about your well-being and we want you to know that you can heal yourself by raising your vibration.

Spend time investing in your personal well-being and do what makes you feel happy. Happiness begins with you, not with your relationships, friends or job. You are your own healer and the medicines you need can be found within the energy around and inside of you. Spend less time seeking to please others and focus more on pleasing yourself.

We want you to know that laughing is the antidote to the situation you are currently in. Laughter can help wash away the problems that you face. Laughter is love, light and healing! When you raise the vibrations of your thoughts and feelings, healing naturally takes place.

Take some time away from the normal busy routine of life so you can focus on your own needs. Detox your body and mind and allow positive energies to surge through you, releasing any negative thoughts from your energy field.

We urge you to take a short break, open some windows or go for a walk and revitalise your body with fresh air.

You are Enough!

We want you to absorb what we are communicating to you, because it is important for your growth and development.

Your feelings are always valid!

A feeling is an experience that can never be wrong and you should learn to honour that! It is your feelings that guide you on your path, so learn to trust them and they will aid you tremendously!

Know that it is safe to enforce your boundaries and let people know when enough is enough. Do remember that it is ok to say *"no"* to things that you are not comfortable with. Receiving other people's approval is not necessary. If you are happy with your decisions, that is all that matters so stick with them!

Do not let anyone's negative thoughts have any power over you, but also remember not to let your own negative thoughts and feelings gain power over what you do! We want you to believe in yourself!

You are all that you need!
You are capable of amazing things!
You are enough!

You Can Do It!

We want you to know that you can do anything when you put your mind, body, heart and soul into it. You are a powerful being of love and light. Lead your life as a positive example to others. If you fall, get back up! You are a warrior!

People around you may criticise or doubt what you say or do, but you can use this as fuel to propel you forward and show them what you are really made of!

Know that you CAN do anything. Anything is possible if you conceive it in your mind first! If you are offered support from people around you, do not be proud or dismiss them. You have the choice to let go of pride, anger or resentment and accept the help that is offered to you if it resonates. This is us supporting and guiding you in your times of need, orchestrating the people to be in the right place at the right time for you.

If there is a new job, project or idea that you feel passionate about, put those thoughts into action. If you have already started something and have not finished it, get it back out and start *operation revival!*

Actions are what get the ball rolling. Nothing will move or change otherwise!

Your Path

You have the power to do what you want! If you want to fly, clear your mind by releasing anything negative or toxic that does not serve you and weighs your beautiful wings down. You were born to fly on this path, not to be dragged down by other people!

Focus on what it is that YOU desire because you have independence in your own wings to take flight to where you choose to go. Remember that your thoughts influence the time it takes for you to get to your destination. Be aware that other people's thoughts, opinions and advice are only an offering. You can absorb what is useful and discard the rest with love and gratitude. You make the ultimate decisions along the path that you travel.

You are the author of your own story. You have the choice to write it the way you want it to go, whilst staying in control and not allowing anyone to influence the way it ends. That is your choice!

The pen you hold to write your story should remain in your hand. Be careful of '*who*' and '*what*' you share with others. If you give your pen away to others, they could potentially be writing your story for you!

Youthfulness

It does not matter how old you are in years, what matters is the youthfulness of your character and inner self!

Do not allow your body, mind and spirit to be limited by your age. You are still young at heart and your time here is still to be enjoyed and relished.

As time goes on, what you enjoy and appreciate continuously changes. You may have enjoyed being more physically adventurous when you were younger, but you now prefer peaceful walks or staying at home. And that is okay. It does not mean you are *'old'*, it simply means that your palate has changed.

The real fountain of youth is to have a pure heart and lead from your authentic self! It is your mind, talents and creativity that you bring to the table that changes the dynamics of life.

Know that whatever your age, there's always room for dreams and ambitions or to develop yourself and the world around you. Never give up or allow time to stop you!

Fresh Air

If you feel down, lost or demotivated, take time out to disconnect and recharge your batteries. Open some windows, go for a walk and let the abundance of fresh air revitalize you.

Your mind, body, spirit and soul need some fresh air to heal, rejuvenate and ground your beautiful being! Spend time absorbing yourself in and around nature.

Connect with everything around you; smell, see, feel and hear the beauty in nature that surrounds you. Breathe it into your soul and feel the increase in energy levels. This will open your mind and offer you a fresh perspective.

Spending time in nature is an abundant source of healing that costs you nothing but your time. Investing your time in nature will raise your vibration and is the greatest force for your wellbeing.

You can also switch off from the disturbances of life, toxic situations and people by spending time enjoying your own company. This will give fresh air to your mind because you are silencing the disruptive noise in your head. Sometimes when you disconnect, you reconnect with a stronger signal!

Support

We feel that you need to take some time out to reflect on a situation that you are currently experiencing or something you have been contemplating.

Be aware of the positive people around you who are genuinely overjoyed by your success and are compassionate and empathetic when you are sad. These are the people who deserve a special place in your heart and who you can comfortably surround yourself with. They are there to uplift you and help guide you on the path that you are on, so listen to their advice and help with an open heart.

Anything is possible when you have the right people there to support you. This does not have to be just family, but friends and even strangers too! Pay attention to those people we send on your path to help guide you.

You are divinely supported in this situation and although you feel isolated at times, you are not alone. Feel our loving presence, comfort and support, which will help you on your journey. Know that you have the strength to push forward, breaking the barriers that confine you.

Family

We want you to know that families are like branches on a tree; they grow in different directions but their roots remain as one. Even when you lose people you love, they always remain within your roots. Whenever you miss them, spend time outdoors near a tree to help you reconnect with them and yourself.

Ensure that you are doing what makes you happy, rather than striving to serve and do things for others. This will only burn you out and lower your vibration because you are not in alignment with your true authentic self.

Taking care of yourself is extremely important, as it contributes to your ability in taking care of others. You are the root of your family but you need to be grounded for it to flourish. Remember that family is not always defined by blood, sometimes it's defined by love.

Spend time grounding and connecting to nature and doing what helps you grow. If that means temporarily disengaging, then go with the flow and let it be.

You are your own unique self and you have your own unique branch. Know that it is ok to outgrow what you once were doing and change direction. This is your life so do not be afraid to live it your way and reach the heights that you dream of!

Transition

If you are going through any changes or disruptions in your health, finances or relationships, rest assured that this situation is only temporary.

It is now time for you to transition into a new area of your life. You need to remain grounded and make yourself adaptable to coping with this change.

Sometimes transition happens when you least expect it so be prepared!

Know that transitioning is a continuous process, which enables you to progress and grow, and start fresh chapters in your book of life.

You will find that, in these transitioning periods, you will shed parts of yourself. You will notice that your circle of friends may change but rest assured that this is all part of the transition and the ebb and flow of life.

It is when you are in a transitional period that you start to come alive, breaking the barriers that once constrained you. From a cocoon that was in a dark place, you then become the beautiful butterfly that is ready to soar to new heights! Remember that change can be good too.

Open Your Heart

It is okay to open your heart and let people close to you. Do not allow any previous experiences of pain and suffering become an obstacle in your current relationships.

When you expect love and you are let down, your soul can feel crushed! Fear, anxiety, confusion, pain and disappointment can overwhelm you but If you master the mentality to have no expectations, you will never be disappointed! Finding a place of joy will assist in extinguishing the pain and hurt that you have previously experienced. But to do this, you must first step out of the walls that imprison your heart.

Know that your soul does not always need protecting from love. If you learn to love yourself, you will have all that you need and that will be enough to let your guard down. Always remember that love does not necessarily have to come from others.

Be grateful for everything and everyone already around you and what you possess. But most importantly, look for love within. It is only when you learn to genuinely love yourself and embrace the individual you are that you can put the energy into loving everything and everyone else.

Infinite Love

We want you to know that infinite abundance is available to you. One of the most significant forms of abundance is love.

If you put pressure or expectations on your relationship with yourself or others, this will only deter you from your path!

We want you to be aware that it is possible to create your own heartache by having expectations of others. Remember that love has no expectations. If you do not expect anything in return, you can never be disappointed!

Rely on your wings and the self-love you pour into yourself to give you the independence you need to stand strong. When you embed this into your mind on a daily basis, you will release the conditioning of the expectations put on love. You will become free to enjoy the things for what they are, instead of what society has made you think!

Love is infinite but loving yourself is the greatest revolution! When love has no expectations, rules or limits, love thrives. Remember to apply this wisdom in your life.

You are an infinite being who has the capability to access infinite abundance. Use the power of love to create a life you love.

Love is energy and energy is contagious. You always gain when you give love!

Practice

In order to rise to the challenges that you face, you must be prepared to change and break the habit of self-limiting thoughts, feelings and beliefs.

You build your own reality with your thoughts. Your reality does not create you! However, if you do not practise using your thoughts wisely, it can mould you into someone you are not.

Motivation is what gets you started, and habit is what keeps you going! If you want to change your life, it is important for you to change something daily. The secret to success and growth is in your daily routine.

Get into the habit of practising doing the same thing each day, so you are always moving one step closer towards your goal. Practising gratitude, mindfulness or meditation, will help ground you in breaking those negative thought patterns that can debilitate you. The more you practise and focus on investing in a healthy environment for your mind, the greater the abundance you will receive. Your mind will be less cluttered with thoughts and feelings that do not serve you.

The power of the mind, combined with action, will combust into an explosion of abundance!

Love

We want you to know that we love you, but we want you to love yourself too! When you feel love for yourself, that love will enable the strength and courage your warrior spirit has to transform pain into power!

Take time for self-care by doing something that you love and enjoy. Be mindful of what you say, think, feel, do and eat. They all require attention and awareness so you can flourish.

If something hurts, let it ricochet off you by responding with love. If you harness your emotions in the direction of love, you become more balanced.

If your thoughts and feelings are taking control of you, ground yourself. Inner peace is required in this situation. To find it, silence your mind from distractions. Do not be in a rush to do or say things.

Let any worries bounce off your energetic field and release yourself from the shackles of fear that burdens you. It is then that you will be able to drop the load that weighs you down, so that you can spread your wings and fly in the direction of what you love.

Authentic Self

We want you to find the courage to be authentic. To do this you need to release yourself from everything society and culture has imposed on your beautiful being!

Authenticity is a daily practice of letting go of who you have been conditioned to *think* you are and embracing who you *really* are.

Know that what makes you vulnerable is not a weakness, it is what makes you beautiful, raw and true. Own that vulnerable side that society often labels as a *"weakness"* because we want you to know that it is not! It shows great courage and promotes and facilitates other people to do the same too! As you step into your authentic self, you become a beacon of light to others, helping them feel safe to embrace their true selves.

You are a treasure chest that holds many hidden gems and you are amongst the rarest! When you are living from your authentic self, know that not everyone may like you, but you are growing and transitioning on your path as you should. Be yourself, accept yourself, forgive yourself and value yourself.

When you are in alignment with your true authentic self, abundance and happiness will surge within your remit. You can then bathe in a stream of peace, love and serenity!

Individuality

We want you to know that you are a precious gift to the world
and here for a great purpose. You are a unique individual and
that is your superpower!

You are enough and there is no need for you to imitate or copy
what others are doing. Whether you realise it yet or not, you are
here in this world to be an original, not a copy! Remember to be
led by your true authentic self because this is what makes you
stand in your superpower of individuality.

You are a beacon of light and can reach people in dark places. If
you ever feel like you are in a dark place or feel vulnerable, fill
yourself up with self-love and care. Most importantly, be kind to
yourself.

Know that your vulnerability is a beautiful attribute because you
are having the courage to be seen for the authentic individual
you are. Vulnerability is your greatest measure of courage.
Remember that courage does not mean you do not get scared, it
means you do not allow fear to stop you!

Step outside of your comfort zone and the box that society has
put you in, regain your power and shine your own beautiful
light. Be the unique individual you were designed to be!

Confidence

We have watched you successfully overcome so much and we commend you for this!

We believe in you, but we want you to have confidence and belief in yourself too because that is when the magic starts to happen. You will then grow and transition into a beautiful butterfly!

Know that confidence is not about being better than others, it is about having belief in yourself and not comparing yourself to others.

You are a strong individual and we want to reassure you that you have the courage to speak out and do what it is you want. Confidence thrives from leading from your true authentic self and being honest with what you know, say and do.

Declutter what does not serve you so you feel lighter and can move with grace and ease. The most beautiful thing you can wear is a smile! Think of your smile as your armour of confidence even in the bleakest of days and it will help you march on.

You are a beautiful energy of love and light and the world needs to feel your presence. You were born to shine!

Believe in Yourself

This message of guidance comes to you because this is an ideal time for you to think about what YOU want, as opposed to what others *'want'* or *'expect'* from you.

You are the captain of your own ship and you can steer it in any direction you wish to sail! Why allow insecurity or fear to prohibit you from cruising out of your comfort zone and travelling into the unknown? We want you to know that this is where your adventure begins. Yes, it is on the other side of fear!

It is fear of the unknown that can often keep you earth bound. You have the choice to allow your soul to grow and soar beyond the limits of restrictive thoughts and feelings.

Believe in yourself and your talents, knowing that there are no limits except the limits you place on yourself.

Have faith in what you do, but above all, have faith in yourself. There is something inside of you that is much greater than any obstacle or challenge. Rise above your deep-rooted fears and ride on the wings of faith and trust. And remember, you are never alone, because we are the wings that you ride on!

Focus

Have faith in our capability to lead you to abundance. All that you need is available to you, but you must learn to focus your mind and express your intentions clearly to us.

Spending time focusing on your own individual needs is imperative on your journey. Where focus goes, energy flows! Ensure that you are pouring all the love and energy into yourself first.

Starve your distractions and feed your focus by using mindfulness techniques and incorporating them into your daily life. A clear mind helps you to directly focus on the road ahead.

Practise inhaling abundance into your life and exhaling all negative thoughts and feelings. Only then will the areas of love, work and relationships begin to prosper.

Give gratitude to everything in your life and your circuit will flow in a synchronistic and harmonious state.

Stay focused on whatever you want to do, not allowing self-doubt to hold your mind and heart captive! Whenever you find yourself doubting how far you can go, just remember how far you have come!

Balance

Although the road you travel upon may be difficult, unpleasant, challenging or testing, trust that you can overcome those feelings. Aim to balance your thoughts and feelings to maintain stability and equilibrium. For every bad thought or feeling, cancel it out with a good thought.

Know that your body is a temple, so keep it filled with love and good thoughts. This is a healthy habitat for your soul to live and flourish in. What benefits your soul benefits your life! The more you care for it, the more blessings and abundance you will receive.

Balance is about two things: h*olding on* versus l*etting go.*

Hold onto memories and experiences that lift your soul and make you smile.

If something is no longer positively affecting your life, would it benefit you to let it go? If you do not let go of what is not serving you, will you be able to receive what you truly deserve? With the knowledge that everything you need is on the other side of fear, would you jump?

Taking that leap of faith could benefit you, but only if you balance your thoughts enough to tip the scale and have the confidence to jump!

Rise

We can see that you want to soar above to new heights and that your inner self needs to break free from unhealthy habits, relationships or environments that prevent you from rising.

Love is the key that unlocks the shackles that prevent you from flying. To break free, you need an equal exchange of giving and receiving love. When you feel love for yourself, you come alive. This vibration will radiate and be felt by those around you and returned in kind.

Do not worry about your fears, instead dissolve them with love and light. You are a warrior! You can fight any negative or toxic situations and rise stronger than ever before. Nourish your mind, body and soul with positivity, healthy foods and love.

Rise above the bombardments of any challenges you face and, like a phoenix out of the ashes, you will be reborn!

It is time for you to fly to new, wonderful heights and awaken a new state of being. You can do this, but you may need to drop the heavy baggage that is weighing your precious wings down!

Reward Yourself

Yes, a big angelic high five from us! You have been working hard in all that you do and we want you to relax, unwind and reward yourself!

Give yourself credit for the good choices you have made or the things that you have been doing, however insignificant or small you may think it is. Remember that every action creates a ripple effect far and wide. We have seen these ripples and we are proud of the positive impact that you have had on those around you.

Know that it is okay to celebrate personal achievements, even if it is just getting out of bed in the morning or going to work when you do not want to. No one else may understand what it took for you to accomplish them but know your worth and reward yourself for anything good you have done.

You deserve to reward yourself and a little extra self-love and care will only fuel you further!

Progression

We are here to remind you that you are strong! Stay positive because every step brings you one step closer to your goals! No matter how slow you feel like you are going, remember that you are moving. Every step counts!

Know that it is okay to stop, take a break and do *'nothing'*, but if you get back up you are progressing! A little progress each day adds up to big results. Love the *'work in progress'* that is you!

If you feel like you are drifting, ground yourself and clear your mind so that your heart can communicate to you. Go for a walk, open some windows and allow the fresh air to rejuvenate your mind, body and soul. A clear mind leads to a merry heart!

When change occurs, do not resist it. Resisting change is resisting your growth and we want to see you progress and grow on your journey! You cannot become or do what you want if you remain where you are. See any challenges as an opportunity to progress and grow to a heightened state of wellbeing.

Your life does not improve by chance, it improves by change! Change can be difficult and chaotic, but in the end it will be beautiful and inspiring to yourself and others. Keep on going, you have got this!

Positive Thinking

We want you to know that in order to change your situation or receive what it is you desire, it is imperative that you keep your thoughts saturated in love and gratitude.

If you alter or connect your thoughts to a frequency of positivity, this will align you physically, mentally, emotionally and spiritually. It is then that you will be open to attract an abundance of all that you wish for and desire.

Seek to understand that your thoughts and choice in words have the power to help change your actions and environment around you. Rather than fearing *'what could go wrong'*, instead ask yourself, *'what could go right'*? Yes, you have the power to flip the script at any time!

Go for a walk and spend some time in nature so you can disconnect from everyone and everything around you! Silence your mind and all that distracts you and then try to look at everything from a fresh, positive perspective.

Sometimes all your mind needs is a bit of tender loving care and training! Tame the negative committee in your mind and you will have 20/20 vision to see the path you were born to follow.

Cultivation

We want you to know that your body and mind needs to be cultivated in order to work effectively and efficiently. What you feed your body is just as important as what you feed your mind.

Fertilising your mind with kindness and love, and your body with healthy habits and substances, are vital! When they are both functioning in unison, this will produce a reservoir of energy.

If you have something to start or complete, now is the time to address it. Everything that you have been contemplating, planning or doing will start to come together when action is taken. Your hard work will inevitably pay off and you will start to reap the rewards, but you must have the energy contained within for you to release the energy needed to harvest your intended outcome.

The journey from the start of conception to completion may be challenging but enjoy and embrace every moment by remaining present. Having the determination and patience, whilst learning from the challenges you may face will be an asset to usher you along the way.

Take the necessary steps to start or complete what you set out to do by cultivating what you wish to grow. It is then that you will be rewarded with fruits from the seeds that you have planted!

Rise

We can see that you want to soar above to new heights and
that your inner self needs to break free from unhealthy habits,
relationships or environments that prevent you from rising.

Love is the key that unlocks the shackles that prevent you from
flying. To break free, you need an equal exchange of giving and
receiving love. When you feel love for yourself, you come alive.
This vibration will radiate and be felt by those around you and
returned in kind.

Do not worry about your fears, instead dissolve them with love
and light. You are a warrior! You can fight any negative or toxic
situations and rise stronger than ever before. Nourish your
mind, body and soul with positivity, healthy foods and love.

Rise above the bombardments of any challenges you face and,
like a phoenix out of the ashes, you will be reborn!

It is time for you to fly to new, wonderful heights and awaken
a new state of being. You can do this, but you may need to drop
the heavy baggage that is weighing your precious wings down!

Relationships

We want you to allow faith to be the driving force to receive abundance in your work or relationships. Let go of any financial or relationship worries that you currently hold. Have faith that we will see you through this situation.

Know that we are diligently watching you throughout this process. The stronger your faith, the stronger the relationship becomes and the stronger you magnetise what you want into your life.

Know that good relationships do not just happen overnight; they take time, commitment, perseverance, love and patience. Build upon these daily with those around you and life will become more balanced.

We want you to know that you are never alone, even at times when you feel like you are. If your heart needs companionship, seek friendship and guidance in us and other people who love you like friends or family, but most importantly yourself!

We love you and want to give you the love you require. Commit to what matters the most but know that you are a priority. For relationships to manifest or prosper, you need to maintain your own needs first.

Fill Yourself Up!

Love is the most powerful energy that you need right now. If you are not receiving it, this can deplete your energy. You do not necessarily need to look to others for love but you can look towards yourself and fill yourself with self-care and love instead! You can always rely on your own branches to keep you elevated!

Take time out to do something you enjoy, be that with friends, family or going to a special place on your own. When you fill yourself up with love and give it to yourself, you will be able to pour with the excess love you have preserved!

Be assertive and remember that it is okay to say no to others. You cannot receive what you have not given to yourself. Give yourself love and it will be given back to you. Self-love and care are crucial when you feel depleted!

Shed what no longer serves you, releasing any fears, worries and problems. If you do, you will be fuelled to gravitate towards love, abundance and success.

When you do what you love, your soul becomes content. This is the environment you need to be in to flourish!

Unleashing Love

Love is the most powerful energy known to mankind and you hold the power to unleash it from within your beautiful being! We want you to know that it is not about changing yourself, it is about loving yourself. You do not need anyone else to complete who you are, you can do that yourself!

If you are in a situation that you have been in before and it is impinging on your heart, change needs to occur for you to progress. Reflect upon your past experiences with what is happening now. Notice the similarities and differences and then consider what you could do differently. If something keeps repeating, perhaps deeper lessons need to be learned to help with your spiritual growth.

Love requires hard work, time, commitment and passion.

If you feel like you have a hole in your heart, the only person that can fill and complete it is you!

We feel the pains contained within your heart as they are ours too. We know that your heart needs love, but the greatest gift you can give yourself is to spend more time on loving yourself! It is then that you can break free of any cycles or patterns that are holding you back. That is the magnificent ripple effect of unleashing self-love and care!

Happiness

Finding time for the things that light you up and make you feel happy to be alive is where you need to be! You deserve to be happy and to live a life you are excited about. Do not let others make you forget that.

Anywhere or anything that ignites happy memories and brings an abundance of joy to your soul is the environment you can safely bathe in. We want you to find your happy place and we feel that it is important that you make this your number one priority right now!

Everything you need to help, heal, rejuvenate or motivate you, resides within you internally. There is no need to look externally for it.

Living in the past and observing others can prevent you from reaching happiness. Instead, be in the present moment of now and look within to find the happiness that will navigate you towards your dreams!

Be happy with what you have. Gratitude alone can bring happiness to you because what you give out, you attract, so always be grateful!

Intuition

Yes, your soul knows exactly which way you are meant to go, but you need to release what does not serve you in this current situation so your soul can lead you there! Only then can you be guided by your intuition, rather than other people's negativity, opinions, beliefs and expectations.

Silence your mind from distractions so that you can feel our loving presence and hear your intuition that is built within.

Pay attention to our gentle nudges through signs and synchronicities that we send you to know that we are helping you on your journey.

We also want you to be mindful of your emotions. Ensure that they do not override or interfere with any decisions you need to make. Respond when you are in a calm and collective state so you can articulate yourself more coherently. Be guided by your feelings and led by your calm thoughts and doors of opportunities and reconcilements will transpire.

Intuition is like a muscle; to develop it you must listen! When you have developed the ability to listen, allow it to be your internal compass to always guide you in the right direction!

Music

If you are feeling low or you are struggling to focus, listen to high frequency sounds or music to help stimulate you and heighten your energy to vibrate on a higher level.

Remember that music and sounds can rapidly affect your mood and alter your vibrational frequency. Listen to music that makes you feel empowered, inspired, motivated and uplifted. Singing also helps you feel the vibrations more powerfully within your body.

Music has the power to change your world and the world of others around you, if you learn to feel rather than just hear.

If you are struggling to sleep at night, try and meditate with calm, relaxing music to ease your mind and soothe you to sleep. Through music, meditation and sleep, your body will be able to heal and recover from any stresses that have been troubling you.

Remember that we always send you signs and messages in the music that you listen to or hear around you. Pay attention!

Realign

We want you to know that grounding is essential right now! The energy within your body is like a wheel that is spinning and rotating. We can see that you currently have blockages within this energetic wheel, and we want to help you realign them.

Make sure you are grounding daily by connecting with nature, meditating, holding grounding stones or crystals. Seek out energetical healers to aid the restoration process. Even healers need healing!

Do not lose sight of your purpose by allowing your negative experiences from the past or present pull you down. This will only interfere with your vibration and energetic field.

Know that any challenges you face are happening for a purpose and when you accept this, you will start to grow.

We want you to know that you are a lightworker here to help others learn and grow from your own experiences. That is why you are a warrior of light! You can help them overcome the fears they face and show them a different perspective. However, before you do this, you need to have the energy and capacity within yourself to act upon this.

You have a significant influence on the destinies of many others and it is therefore vital that you are perfectly aligned.

Play

We have been observing you and we want you to know that more time needs to be made for having fun!

We have noticed your mind and body have been working hard lately and your energy levels could do with a boost! Too much work and not enough play is not good for the mind, body or soul.

You cannot give your energy to other people or projects if you do not have enough reserved for yourself. Therefore, it is essential to take time out for yourself and participate in activities that satisfy your soul and help re-energise your being.

When you spend time in a state of "play", you can release the load that burdens your precious being. Spend time being with or around children and release your inner child that is yearning to be set free!

See, feel and listen to the world from the goodness of your heart. Smile, laugh and bask in the ambience of fun! This will open your senses and give you more clarity and direction in your life.

This is what your body requires to restore your energy. When your energy is restored, you become more effective and efficient in everything that you do.

Compassion

We want you to know that every small act of kindness goes a long way. You are here to make an impact in the world but remember sometimes less is more!

Working hard and earning money is not the only way to success. Do not underestimate the power of a hug, smile, a kind word or compliment; a shoulder for someone to cry on or a listening ear. They can have the potential to turn someone's whole life around.

Compassion not only helps others rise but it also helps you too. If you want to be happy and turn your life around, try practising compassion with yourself too! Here is our extra nudge of guidance to you:

Consider reducing the food, people or environments that deplete your energy and leave you feeling tired, frustrated, or low.

Add some fun, adventure and happiness into your life as part of your daily routine.

Relax and rejuvenate your mind and body by disconnecting with technology for at least half an hour before going to bed.

Engage with us and connect with mother nature by getting some fresh air and re-connecting back to source.

Have compassion for yourself, by taking **CARE** of you!

Time Management

We feel that now is the time for some quiet reflection. When you know how to silence what distracts you, it is then that you become more aware of where and how you can better use your time.

Stop saying: '*I don't have time to do things*' or '*there's not enough time in the day*', as you are only creating obstacles for yourself! Consider where you can adjust things to create more time. It is up to you to invest your time into what is important to you. No one else is responsible for this but you.

Write down what you need to do and organise a structured plan of how and when you will do this. You can then effectively manage your own time and expectations, as well as others.

It is important to include time for yourself and your loved ones. When you balance your time with the needs of yourself, you become more focused and ready to face each day.

Faith

We surround and comfort you with a blanket of love and strength. Hold onto it tight and feel secure in the presence of our unconditional love. Faith is invisible, but it has the power to connect you to what you need.

Allow your faith and love to be bigger and stronger than your fears. Fear is an energy that contracts and love is an energy that expands. Envision a bright, white light encompassing your being whenever you feel deflated or like you want to give up. Love is light and this is what will help you expand!

Your faith can shift any obstacles but be mindful that your fears can also generate them. Let go of anything that weighs you down and do not doubt yourself! If doubt creeps in, inhale confidence and exhale fear.

You can change the scene of your life at any time from the energy around you. Spend time reconnecting with us and nature, drawing these harmonious energies into your soul.

Know that faith resides within your heart and it will give you the strength you need to take that next step. Have faith in yourself and trust that you have the power to overcome and do anything! If you see 222 or 2222, that is a direct message of guidance from us to remind you to *"Keep the Faith!"*

111 Intentions

If you see 111, know that we are encouraging you to wake up, pay attention and align yourself to an elevated thought frequency. This page serves as a reminder that you can manifest anything into your reality. If you think about your intentions, feel it and believe it, your thoughts will create all that you wish.

Before you go to bed and upon awakening, you can programme your subconscious mind with what you desire, as if you have already acquired it. A habit of doing this daily will transport this into your reality.

You create your reality by the thoughts and seeds that you plant but you must nourish them daily, watering them with feelings of faith, love and joy. If you focus on what you want, your power of intention will intensify with great speed. Always remember that your thoughts hold significant power!

Self-Love

This message of guidance we give you serves as an important reminder for you to look after yourself more. It is necessary for you to cultivate your growth, by watering yourself with the love that you need.

We need you to know that you are important and that seeing yourself as a priority is essential on the path you walk on, especially for your progression. It is necessary for you to make sure that you are spending enough time on yourself. The love you give to yourself is the love that you will receive back, and your soul thrives on this.

Your body is a vehicle of love and light, but you cannot arrive at your destination if your tank is not filled up! You cannot give to others what you have not got yourself. Fill yourself up with love, joy and peace and your heart will be open to receive.

It is when you wholeheartedly feel the unconditional love for yourself that you can become a beacon of light for others and truly put the energy into loving everything else.

The relationship you have with yourself sets the tone for the relationships around you. Remember that love must start with you first!

Intuition

Yes, your soul knows exactly which way you are meant to go, but you need to release what does not serve you in this current situation so your soul can lead you there! Only then can you be guided by your intuition, rather than other people's negativity, opinions, beliefs and expectations.

Silence your mind from distractions so that you can feel our loving presence and hear your intuition that is built within.

Pay attention to our gentle nudges through signs and synchronicities that we send you to know that we are helping you on your journey.

We also want you to be mindful of your emotions. Ensure that they do not override or interfere with any decisions you need to make. Respond when you are in a calm and collective state so you can articulate yourself more coherently. Be guided by your feelings and led by your calm thoughts and doors of opportunities and reconcilements will transpire.

Intuition is like a muscle; to develop it you must listen! When you have developed the ability to listen, allow it to be your internal compass to always guide you in the right direction!

Energy & Vibration

You can create abundance with the power of your mind but be aware when your mind is acting like a yo-yo and your thoughts are up and down. This is a sign that you need to stop!

Allowing negative thoughts to dominate your mind will only attract negativity back towards you. Allowing anxiety, doubt, fear and worry to distract you, will lower your vibrations! Instead, focus your energy in being with people who you love and make you feel happy and content. Maintain this state of mind and you will open a gateway for abundance to flow through.

Put your time and energy into setting your intentions with belief and hope. Visualise what it is that you want. Feel it, believe it and imagine receiving it. The positive vibrations of energy that you emit, you will attract!

Once your mind is released from the prison of your thoughts, you will be more open to obtain what you desire because you are vibrating at a higher frequency. Your thoughts and words are a vibration of energy. You must learn to change them so you are vibrating on a harmonious frequency to support what it is you want to receive.

Remember, the raw capability of the mind is limitless!

You are Enough!

We want you to absorb what we are communicating to you, because it is important for your growth and development.

Your feelings are always valid!

A feeling is an experience that can never be wrong and you should learn to honour that! It is your feelings that guide you on your path, so learn to trust them and they will aid you tremendously!

Know that it is safe to enforce your boundaries and let people know when enough is enough. Do remember that it is ok to say "*no*" to things that you are not comfortable with. Receiving other people's approval is not necessary. If you are happy with your decisions, that is all that matters so stick with them!

Do not let anyone's negative thoughts have any power over you, but also remember not to let your own negative thoughts and feelings gain power over what you do! We want you to believe in yourself!

You are all that you need!
You are capable of amazing things!
You are enough!

Notice the Signs

We want you to slow down so that you can notice the signs we send you. Look out for number sequences, feathers, dimes, robins, hummingbirds, rainbows and ladybirds. These are all signs you are on the right track and that you are being guided by us and any loved ones who have passed away.

We also want you to be aware of what other people are going through. Remember, you notice more when you are silent and observing. Think before you speak or react. This is our wisdom to you.

If you notice any signs of pain, negativity or anger in others, tap into your compassionate nature to help them but make sure you do not absorb their feelings or energy. As an empathic soul, it is crucial that you protect your energy by firmly grounding yourself.

You can also help those who are suffering through prayer, intention or meditation by sending them love and light. This will also help you with your own healing and growth as well as theirs. When you are serving others through the eyes of love and compassion, you receive that love and healing back to yourself as well.

Self-Love

This message of guidance we give you serves as an important reminder for you to look after yourself more. It is necessary for you to cultivate your growth, by watering yourself with the love that you need.

We need you to know that you are important and that seeing yourself as a priority is essential on the path you walk on, especially for your progression. It is necessary for you to make sure that you are spending enough time on yourself. The love you give to yourself is the love that you will receive back, and your soul thrives on this.

Your body is a vehicle of love and light, but you cannot arrive at your destination if your tank is not filled up! You cannot give to others what you have not got yourself. Fill yourself up with love, joy and peace and your heart will be open to receive.

It is when you wholeheartedly feel the unconditional love for yourself that you can become a beacon of light for others and truly put the energy into loving everything else.

The relationship you have with yourself sets the tone for the relationships around you. Remember that love must start with you first!

Infinite Love

We want you to know that infinite abundance is available to you. One of the most significant forms of abundance is love.

If you put pressure or expectations on your relationship with yourself or others, this will only deter you from your path!

We want you to be aware that it is possible to create your own heartache by having expectations of others. Remember that love has no expectations. If you do not expect anything in return, you can never be disappointed!

Rely on your wings and the self-love you pour into yourself to give you the independence you need to stand strong. When you embed this into your mind on a daily basis, you will release the conditioning of the expectations put on love. You will become free to enjoy the things for what they are, instead of what society has made you think!

Love is infinite but loving yourself is the greatest revolution! When love has no expectations, rules or limits, love thrives. Remember to apply this wisdom in your life.

You are an infinite being who has the capability to access infinite abundance. Use the power of love to create a life you love.

Love is energy and energy is contagious. You always gain when you give love!

Success

This page is a sign that magnified abundance and success is on its way. All roads that lead to success require self-belief and hard work, but we want you to balance this by taking time out for yourself too.

Know that behind every successful person there have been many challenges, mistakes and failures. Be kind to yourself and know that all of these serve a purpose, even though it may not feel like it at the time.

Be aware of unexpected openings and opportunities that are offered to you. Do not let them pass you by because of fear or anxiety. Dissolve your fears by creating an image of a butterfly in your mind, blow it into your hand and then release your worries or uncertainties by blowing it out with love and light and visualising them fluttering away!

Let your imagination and creativity lead you to the fortune and dreams that you crave. It is then that your hard work and dedication will pay off and you will reap the rewards of the seeds that you have sown.

Support

We feel that you need to take some time out to reflect on a
situation that you are currently experiencing or something you
have been contemplating.

Be aware of the positive people around you who are genuinely
overjoyed by your success and are compassionate and
empathetic when you are sad. These are the people who deserve
a special place in your heart and who you can comfortably
surround yourself with. They are there to uplift you and help
guide you on the path that you are on, so listen to their advice
and help with an open heart.

Anything is possible when you have the right people there to
support you. This does not have to be just family, but friends
and even strangers too! Pay attention to those people we send on
your path to help guide you.

You are divinely supported in this situation and although
you feel isolated at times, you are not alone. Feel our loving
presence, comfort and support, which will help you on your
journey. Know that you have the strength to push forward,
breaking the barriers that confine you.

Fill Yourself Up!

Love is the most powerful energy that you need right now. If you are not receiving it, this can deplete your energy. You do not necessarily need to look to others for love but you can look towards yourself and fill yourself with self-care and love instead! You can always rely on your own branches to keep you elevated!

Take time out to do something you enjoy, be that with friends, family or going to a special place on your own. When you fill yourself up with love and give it to yourself, you will be able to pour with the excess love you have preserved!

Be assertive and remember that it is okay to say no to others. You cannot receive what you have not given to yourself. Give yourself love and it will be given back to you. Self-love and care are crucial when you feel depleted!

Shed what no longer serves you, releasing any fears, worries and problems. If you do, you will be fuelled to gravitate towards love, abundance and success.

When you do what you love, your soul becomes content. This is the environment you need to be in to flourish!

Soul Guidance

Your experiences and circumstances are both connected. These things do not define you but mould and prepare you for your journey ahead.

It may feel like you are isolated and alone at times but know that this can help you navigate towards your soul's purpose. Sometimes when you lose friendships or relationships, you find yourself on a different path and it is here that you may discover your passion and purpose.

Block the thoughts of what others think you '*should*' do, otherwise your feelings of what you '*want*' to do become obstructed. Remember, it is your passion that will lead you towards your purpose, not others.

Your soul is your definitive guidance system. It acts as a compass, map and destination, all in one. Listen to your intuition; this is your soul's guidance. It can be heard when the mind is calm and disengaged from the distractions around you.

We want you to know that whenever you feel lost, down or in despair, turn inwards! When you enter the silence of your soul, you can ask for healing and guidance on your path. You are your own passport home!

Practice

In order to rise to the challenges that you face, you must be prepared to change and break the habit of self-limiting thoughts, feelings and beliefs.

You build your own reality with your thoughts. Your reality does not create you! However, if you do not practise using your thoughts wisely, it can mould you into someone you are not.

Motivation is what gets you started, and habit is what keeps you going! If you want to change your life, it is important for you to change something daily. The secret to success and growth is in your daily routine.

Get into the habit of practising doing the same thing each day, so you are always moving one step closer towards your goal. Practising gratitude, mindfulness or meditation, will help ground you in breaking those negative thought patterns that can debilitate you. The more you practise and focus on investing in a healthy environment for your mind, the greater the abundance you will receive. Your mind will be less cluttered with thoughts and feelings that do not serve you.

The power of the mind, combined with action, will combust into an explosion of abundance!

Another page is calling you...
Go back 3 pages
or
Go forward 3 pages

Change

Change is on the horizon and it is to be embraced! Know that this change will benefit you in the long term, even if it feels like an uphill battle.

If you feel like you are struggling, we will send you a direct message of 555 or 5555 on your path. This is a reminder from us that this change is here to benefit your soul! Keep the faith!

We want you to be open to change, starting with yourself. Change occurs in stages within the mind. When you alter your thoughts, it adds more depth at each phase. The result will be the beautiful transformation of yourself and all that you desire from what you have created in your mind.

Know that you cannot change other people, but you can change your behaviour, attitude and actions. If you want a different result, try making a different choice for change to occur. Regardless of what happens, your choice will always serve to benefit you in the long run.

Sometimes your life needs to be turned upside down, shaken and changed to relocate you to the exact place you need to be. Everything happens for a reason. Trust the process; we have got your back!

Organisation

We want you to invest in your time wisely. Organisation will help in shortening the road to your goals and dreams and reduce stress and clutter in the process. This will save you time and money, thus giving you a better quality of life and more freedom to grow and move in different directions.

Remember that organising or cleaning is a practise. Stay on top of it, being mindful not to get complacent because this will only deplete your time and energy further down the line. Being organised requires discipline; if you practice this every day it will become a habit that will aid you in your everyday life.

When you organise your environment and mind, you release all the clutter that does not serve you. This disarray, chaos and imbalance affects your energy and can block you from moving forward on the path of abundance and opportunities.

Organisation enables you to manage and take control of your life and have clarity in all that you see and do. Remember that a tidy space is a tidy mind!

Adjustments

If you are feeling like there is a block to the stream of abundance, finances, or the love that you receive, then you need to reflect upon your current situation and adjust accordingly.

If the problems are within your relationships, family or work life, then change needs to occur from within. Accept that you cannot change other people, but know you *can* alter what you are currently doing.

Most of the stress that you face can arise from the way you or others respond. You can choose to respond by walking away, saying nothing or adjusting your attitude and that additional stress will gradually disperse. It can also prevent unnecessary confrontations from occurring.

When you feel like you do not like the direction you are going in, adjust your sails and redirect. When you master the habit of adjustment, you will see that it is better to bend a little than to break a solid foundation or loving relationship. If things get rough, have faith in us to guide and coast you through the storm until you get to still waters.

Adjustment is not easy, but see this situation as an adventure where all the obstacles you face are mere challenges. It is like climbing up a mountain; it takes time, hard work and perseverance, but when you get to the top, you will be able to reward yourself for your achievements!

Gratitude

We want you to know that the life you are currently living is like a mirror. It reflects your thoughts, feelings and actions.

Get into a habit of having uplifting thoughts in the morning and before you go to bed. This can change your whole day.

Ingraining daily gratitude into your thoughts each day is important to raise your energy and vibration. The more gratitude you give, the more things you will receive to be grateful for!

Focus on seeing the light at the end of a tunnel when times are a little low or rocky. When you acknowledge all the things that you already have in your life, these acknowledgements will build the foundation for the abundance that you will receive. The more gratitude you express, the stronger that foundation becomes!

Gratitude is a tool that can be used to maintain your physical, mental and spiritual wellbeing. It is the best medicine, for it heals your mind, body and soul. Expressing gratitude, either verbally or written down, is your vitamin for the soul!

Gratitude is like a boomerang; what you throw out into the universe will always come back to you in some shape or form!

Assertiveness

This reading serves as a reminder to be more assertive when you need to be. Know that it is okay to say *"no"* sometimes. Why say yes to things at the cost of your own happiness?

It is time to concentrate on yourself, to do what needs to be done to move forward and reach your intended destination. You need to focus on thinking about your own needs more and not putting other people's needs first. Having the courage to be honest and open with other people and yourself is essential for your progression.

Getting caught up worrying about other people's opinions or beliefs will not always benefit your progression. Be aware of external factors that may affect any decisions that you make. Allowing or absorbing what others dictate to you will not serve you in the long-term.

Instead, rely on your own expertise and knowledge and apply what you know or feel to the situation, instead of asking for someone else's opinion.

Talk to yourself sometimes, when you need expert advice!

Time

The time that you have is precious and we often see it being wasted. We want you to take the time to reflect upon this...

Ask yourself who and what you are spending your time on? Think about those who might be depleting your time and energy. Consider whether your time might be better served with those that add value to your life.

Heed our words of loving wisdom...
Time costs nothing, but it is valuable and priceless!
You cannot possess it, but you can benefit from it.
You cannot keep time, but you can spend it.
Once you have lost it, you can never get it back!

If you are chasing money for happiness, why not chase happiness and let money flow to you from doing what you love?

Time is not only measured by the hands on a clock but also by your internal rhythm and a collection of your experiences and memories. The reason we urge you to spend your time more wisely is to ensure you continuously experience life in alignment with what benefits you. This keeps your daily rhythm beating on a happy, content note.

Technology

We would like to see you and your loved ones disconnect from, what we perceive to be, the needless desire and addiction of using technology. You need to reconnect with who you are, what you truly require and what you have right in front of you.

We have observed that technology is like a drug, consuming and wasting much time and energy that could be better used elsewhere. When you are out, look around you rather than looking down at your technological device and see what everyone else is doing.

Do you want to be part of this system, or do you want to be free to release yourself from these shackles that confine you and the loved ones around you? The choice is ultimately yours!

Spend less time using technology and more time enjoying and appreciating the people and things around you.

Beyond your phone and laptop there is a beautiful world waiting for you to experience the endless wonders it has to offer. Go out and play!

Self-Worth

Self-worth is vital for your wellbeing and happiness. If you do not feel good about yourself, how can you feel good about anything or anyone else?

Know your worth and do not settle for less than you deserve! Why allow people at work or in relationships to treat you inadequately, just because you love them or because of what they have done for you? Remember you do not owe anybody anything!

We want you to know that you do not need to find your self-worth in other people, you can only find it within yourself. It is then that you will be able to attract a job or relationship that is worthy of you! Work on being in love with the person that you see in the mirror, that person who has been through so much and is still standing!

Nobody is entitled to treat you less than your worth. If they do, learn to walk away or distance yourself from them because they will only continue holding you down and suppressing the beautiful being that you are.

Do not allow anyone to dull your beautiful sparkle, you were born to shine!

Soul Guidance

Your experiences and circumstances are both connected. These things do not define you but mould and prepare you for your journey ahead.

It may feel like you are isolated and alone at times but know that this can help you navigate towards your soul's purpose. Sometimes when you lose friendships or relationships, you find yourself on a different path and it is here that you may discover your passion and purpose.

Block the thoughts of what others think you '*should*' do, otherwise your feelings of what you '*want*' to do become obstructed. Remember, it is your passion that will lead you towards your purpose, not others.

Your soul is your definitive guidance system. It acts as a compass, map and destination, all in one. Listen to your intuition; this is your soul's guidance. It can be heard when the mind is calm and disengaged from the distractions around you.

We want you to know that whenever you feel lost, down or in despair, turn inwards! When you enter the silence of your soul, you can ask for healing and guidance on your path. You are your own passport home!

Technology

We would like to see you and your loved ones disconnect from, what we perceive to be, the needless desire and addiction of using technology. You need to reconnect with who you are, what you truly require and what you have right in front of you.

We have observed that technology is like a drug, consuming and wasting much time and energy that could be better used elsewhere. When you are out, look around you rather than looking down at your technological device and see what everyone else is doing.

Do you want to be part of this system, or do you want to be free to release yourself from these shackles that confine you and the loved ones around you? The choice is ultimately yours!

Spend less time using technology and more time enjoying and appreciating the people and things around you.

Beyond your phone and laptop there is a beautiful world waiting for you to experience the endless wonders it has to offer. Go out and play!

You are Enough!

We want you to absorb what we are communicating to you, because it is important for your growth and development.

Your feelings are always valid!

A feeling is an experience that can never be wrong and you should learn to honour that! It is your feelings that guide you on your path, so learn to trust them and they will aid you tremendously!

Know that it is safe to enforce your boundaries and let people know when enough is enough. Do remember that it is ok to say *"no"* to things that you are not comfortable with. Receiving other people's approval is not necessary. If you are happy with your decisions, that is all that matters so stick with them!

Do not let anyone's negative thoughts have any power over you, but also remember not to let your own negative thoughts and feelings gain power over what you do! We want you to believe in yourself!

You are all that you need!
You are capable of amazing things!
You are enough!

New Beginnings

We want you to remain patient. You are soon to be offered a new beginning, opportunity or fresh start.

No matter how old you are, you are still capable of starting new ventures and trying new experiences. Remember that sometimes some things must come to an end for a new doorway of opportunity to open. Let go of anything that no longer serves you or adds any benefit to your life and embrace what is to come.

You will experience new feelings and emotions when you begin this new chapter in your life. It may take time to adapt to, but embrace this new change with patience and trust!

We will send people to support and guide you through this transition, so be aware and mindful of the wisdom that they bring you. Wisdom is a beautiful thing as you can draw upon different aspects of other people's lives. This is a beautiful gift!

Have faith in your dreams and do not let anyone infiltrate their negativity into your field of happiness. Embrace and accept your own individuality and strengths. This is your time to shine and be who you want to be!

Patience

We can see your frustration in a specific area of your life and we want you to know we are supporting you. Trust in us and have patience.

Patience is not about the ability to wait, but the attitude you have whilst waiting! Build a relationship by communicating daily to your inner and outer needs and take the time to nurture them. You do not necessarily need a mind that is speaking, but a patient heart that is listening. It is then that the insight and support you require will be presented to you.

Learn to accept that things can happen in different ways, rather than the ways that you expect. Everything happens for a divine reason and everything is coming together as it should to benefit you in the best way possible.

Have faith that opportunities and abundance will soon be presented to you. Do not allow your faith to waiver. Worry and fear ends where faith begins. Remain patient and know that everything comes in divine timing. Trust in us.

The best things in life are worth waiting for!

Positive Thinking

We want you to know that in order to change your situation or receive what it is you desire, it is imperative that you keep your thoughts saturated in love and gratitude.

If you alter or connect your thoughts to a frequency of positivity, this will align you physically, mentally, emotionally and spiritually. It is then that you will be open to attract an abundance of all that you wish for and desire.

Seek to understand that your thoughts and choice in words have the power to help change your actions and environment around you. Rather than fearing *'what could go wrong'*, instead ask yourself, *'what could go right'*? Yes, you have the power to flip the script at any time!

Go for a walk and spend some time in nature so you can disconnect from everyone and everything around you! Silence your mind and all that distracts you and then try to look at everything from a fresh, positive perspective.

Sometimes all your mind needs is a bit of tender loving care and training! Tame the negative committee in your mind and you will have 20/20 vision to see the path you were born to follow.

Happiness

Finding time for the things that light you up and make you feel happy to be alive is where you need to be! You deserve to be happy and to live a life you are excited about. Do not let others make you forget that.

Anywhere or anything that ignites happy memories and brings an abundance of joy to your soul is the environment you can safely bathe in. We want you to find your happy place and we feel that it is important that you make this your number one priority right now!

Everything you need to help, heal, rejuvenate or motivate you, resides within you internally. There is no need to look externally for it.

Living in the past and observing others can prevent you from reaching happiness. Instead, be in the present moment of now and look within to find the happiness that will navigate you towards your dreams!

Be happy with what you have. Gratitude alone can bring happiness to you because what you give out, you attract, so always be grateful!

Direction

We feel that there is a deep need for you to contemplate the route you want to travel along, letting your heart navigate you.

We want you to recognise that direction is more important than the speed you are travelling at. You hold the key to your vehicle in your heart and mind, but first you must have faith and trust in the route you envision. If you can see it, feel it and believe it, the path ahead will become much clearer.

At points on your journey you will need to rely on your own intuition and independence. If travelling alone makes you feel fearful or anxious, know that the journey you face unaccompanied can also make you the strongest! Remember, walking alone is sometimes better than walking with people who do not value you!

Remember, you are in control of the steering wheel. You decide which direction you want to go in!

Have faith that the journey you are on is destined for you and has a purpose, however tough it may seem. Know that there are no bad decisions, as there are always lessons to be learnt from every situation. Keep moving, one foot in front of the other. Small steps are better than no steps!

Perseverance

No matter how hard the road ahead may seem, you must keep moving forward. Remember that forward is forward, however slow you go!

We are cheering you on, so keep pushing yourself in the direction of your purpose and soul calling! Believe in yourself and push through the limits that you or others place in your way. Tough situations build strong people!

Do not give up, even when you feel like you want to. The world loves a stubborn heart. If you fall or make mistakes, it is okay, you can still get back up! We believe in you.

Never think that you are a failure. You only fail when you stop trying! We are ushering, nudging and shaking you to move forward and keep going! You can do this!

If things are really draining your energy, take a break to relax and re-energise and then get back on the path you were walking. You may not have reached your destination just yet, but you are closer than you were yesterday.

Remember to be kind to yourself and do not be disheartened. It is often the last key in the bunch that opens the door to where you want to enter!

New Project

We want you to know that this is your life to live the way you want. You are in control of your own destiny!

If there is a new project you want to start or continue and you are feeling blocked or demotivated, take a step back to reflect. Consider what you feel is preventing you from growing and what you need to do to move forward. If it helps, write this down on a piece of paper so that you can see a clear structure on how to start or progress.

Focus on the end goal you wish to actualise and hold this clearly in your mind. Let go of any worries or concerns about how you are going to get there and trust that everything will work out.

No matter what your current circumstance is, if you are able to imagine something that sparks a light within your soul, you will be able to create something better for yourself.

Embrace your individuality within this new project and you will succeed in anything you do. There is no one else in the world like you and that is your unique power! Do not follow other people's footprints or path. Instead, create your own.

Protection

Have courage to stand firm and hold your space in order to protect your energy field. Be aware that holding onto pride, resentment or anger can potentially prevent you from expanding. Holding onto these qualities is like holding onto a hot piece of coal with the intention of throwing it at someone else, but the only person who will get burnt is you!

In order to prevent you from absorbing negativity, getting hurt or lowering your energy and vibration, release anything that does not serve you.

Shield and protect yourself by visualising a pure white bubble of love and light around you, especially when in toxic environments or when you are feeling depleted. We are always here to protect you and give you an extra shield of protection when you call upon us in this way!

Know that love can penetrate the field of negativity and darkness in your life, but remember that darkness CANNOT penetrate love and light!

You are a Warrior of Light and here for a divine purpose! Have faith that you can withstand any storm. Visualise yourself with an armour of love placed upon you, so you are ready to enter any situation that you may face with courage and valour!

Invest in Yourself

We want to support you in fulfilling your potential. Spending time worrying about who likes or dislikes you will potentially deter you from your purpose. When you invest in your own thoughts, happiness will follow.

Life is a journey of ups and downs but you hold the key to create the life you desire. Happiness, love, success and dreams are all yours for the taking, but you must use the key to unlock those treasures. The key to doing this will be released when you learn to make yourself a priority. Self- love and care are imperative in the journey you embark upon. Self-love is not a selfish act but a necessary one!

Invest in filling yourself up with self-love and care because your life purpose is much greater than you know. You need to be optimising at full capacity to achieve all it is you intend on accomplishing. Listen to the whispers of what your body, heart, mind and soul need and then act upon them.

Invest your time, passion and commitment to your visions and goals and you will soon reap the rewards. The amount of energy you put in is what you will receive, but do not forget the greatest investment to propel forward is in yourself!

Purpose

Know that everyone discovers their soul purpose at different stages of their lives and this is orchestrated divinely! If you know your soul purpose, do not lose sight of it. Know that every 'bad' day serves a purpose and aids you in your progression.

If you do not know or fully understand your soul purpose yet, do not worry. Everything will unfold as and when it should. Everything happens when it is intended; trust the process and keep moving forwards.

Know that your path is not always a straight line sometimes there are twists and turns along the way. If you go down the *'wrong'* road and you get *'lost'*, do not worry. You may think you are lost, but you could be exactly where you need to be and perhaps about to discover something significant to aid you on your journey in the future. Remember, everything happens for a reason!

The experiences you have endured so far have taught you valuable lessons to help you grow. Your strength arises from the continuous efforts and struggles that you have overcome. We have watched and supported you throughout these times and we are proud of your achievements.

Grounding

We know that you want to feel free and fly high in everything you do but we want you to know that in order to fly, you must start from the ground. The more grounded you are, the higher you will fly.

It is through practise, patience and perseverance that you will begin to navigate through any storms you may face on your path. If you are feeling all over the place, use some of these grounding techniques to help you:

-Walk barefooted, connecting with mother nature.
-Hug a tree or meditate underneath one.
-Visualise yourself either under a tree connecting to the roots or even better, be the tree!
-Wade in water, fill your lungs with fresh air by going for a walk or opening your windows.

Raise your face to the warmth of the sun and connect with the fire. Raise your face to the bright, shining moon and connect with the light. It is then that you will feel and absorb the vast power and energy within your very being!

Nature does not just ground you, it also nourishes, heals and transforms you. It helps you to grow and blossom into the beautiful being you were designed to be!

Courage

We are here to give you the strength and courage you need so you do not resist the changes that are unravelling in your life. These changes are here to help you evolve and grow, not to create a feeling of being stuck or paralysed. Gather and receive the strength that we send you and stand tall to whatever comes your way.

Have the courage to make the changes you need and the strength to see them through. You can do this! You are strong! Even though it may feel like everything around you could be falling apart, perhaps it is really falling into place. We see this and in time you will too.

It takes great strength to stand alone! We admire and love this quality you possess. Your individuality brings you the gift of freedom and flight. It takes great courage to become who you are, and for this you will be rewarded with great abundance.

Remember to maintain the connection with yourself by staying in the present moment of now. Remain balanced, grounded and aware so that you have the clarity to summon the power of strength and courage that dwells within your beautiful soul.

You have a warrior spirit. Do not allow your past to define you.

Your past does not define your destiny!

Service

You will notice that others around you will become more drawn to you to seek your help and guidance. Use your experiences and inner wisdom to help them. The tools you have are all within you, trust in your instincts to guide your words.

Always remember that helping others also helps yourself because you rise when you lift others up, consequently shifting your energy to vibrate on a higher level. When you lose yourself in the service of others, you will discover your own happiness and understand what makes your own light shine brighter.

Be aware of your boundaries and learn to recognise when your energy starts to become too depleted. It is good to help others but make sure you find the right balance. Remember to always look after yourself too.

You cannot give to others if you have not given to yourself first. Feed yourself with an abundance of self-love and care and declutter what does not serve you.

We are a divine source and we are always here to help you, should you need any guidance. Just call upon us and we will always answer your call.

Adjustments

If you are feeling like there is a block to the stream of abundance, finances, or the love that you receive, then you need to reflect upon your current situation and adjust accordingly.

If the problems are within your relationships, family or work life, then change needs to occur from within. Accept that you cannot change other people, but know you *can* alter what you are currently doing.

Most of the stress that you face can arise from the way you or others respond. You can choose to respond by walking away, saying nothing or adjusting your attitude and that additional stress will gradually disperse. It can also prevent unnecessary confrontations from occurring.

When you feel like you do not like the direction you are going in, adjust your sails and redirect. When you master the habit of adjustment, you will see that it is better to bend a little than to break a solid foundation or loving relationship. If things get rough, have faith in us to guide and coast you through the storm until you get to still waters.

Adjustment is not easy, but see this situation as an adventure where all the obstacles you face are mere challenges. It is like climbing up a mountain; it takes time, hard work and perseverance, but when you get to the top, you will be able to reward yourself for your achievements!

Contemplation

If you feel like you have come to a standstill in a specific area of your life or are currently stalling, contemplate on what could be holding you back.

Reflect upon your past and present circumstances and unearth any potential knowledge or expertise that will help you move forward. Remind yourself of the love that is or was once around you. Feel and breathe in the memories and harness that love to move you forward in your situation.

The road you are on may sometimes feel uncertain, but at least you are on a road. You just need to decide which direction you want to go. Trust your intuition for it guides you well.

We want you to know that to achieve anything externally, you must first contemplate changing how you think and feel internally. If you change your focus and let go of what does not serve your highest good, you create space for fulfilment to enter your life. The road ahead then becomes much clearer.

Start each day with gratitude and love. In return you will be blessed with all that you need. When you operate like a magnet, you will attract everything that matches your frequency. Now that is something serious to contemplate on!

Acceptance

We can see that there is a great need for accepting what has happened in the past and releasing everything that is weighing down on your precious wings! Know that nobody's life is *'perfect'*. What you perceive in others as the *'perfect'* life may not be the case behind closed doors! We say this with a wink...
"Never judge a book by its cover."

When you accept that you are perfect just the way you are and that you will always have challenges, you will slowly be able to release the load that is pulling you down.

Learn to recognise that every situation aids your growth. When you do, you will surely flourish! When you place expectations on yourself, relationships or work, you limit the progress of your growth.

Remember that:
'Good people' bring you the gift of love, happiness and memories. Who you consider to be *'bad people'*, bring you the gift of experiences and lessons. Both facets can aid your growth. Every person that crosses your path is therefore a blessing and sometimes in disguise!

Accept everything for the positivity that it can bring and you will lead a positive and abundant life. This is because you will be able to accept things for what they *are* rather than for what you *think* they should be!

111 Intentions

If you see 111, know that we are encouraging you to wake up, pay attention and align yourself to an elevated thought frequency. This page serves as a reminder that you can manifest anything into your reality. If you think about your intentions, feel it and believe it, your thoughts will create all that you wish.

Before you go to bed and upon awakening, you can programme your subconscious mind with what you desire, as if you have already acquired it. A habit of doing this daily will transport this into your reality.

You create your reality by the thoughts and seeds that you plant but you must nourish them daily, watering them with feelings of faith, love and joy. If you focus on what you want, your power of intention will intensify with great speed. Always remember that your thoughts hold significant power!

Unison

When you are feeling downhearted or confused, it could be because your heart and mind are not working in harmony. Unity is strength and when the heart and mind work in unison, wonderful things can be achieved. Your body and soul will then gravitate towards love and joy.

In order to form in unison, fill your mind with gratitude and joyful memories that make you laugh or smile. Go for walks and breathe in the fresh air to rejuvenate your weary soul. When you are feeling lost, connecting and spending time in nature will help you find yourself again.

A lot has changed and will continue to change around you, and because of this, so will you! You are ready to come out of the cocoon that you are currently hibernating in so you can transform into a stronger and wiser being.

Cherish and appreciate what you have at present and what you have received. If you have lost something, think about the experiences, lessons and wisdom it brought you. It is when you choose to focus on the good things you have in your life rather than the things you do not have, that you begin to work in unison with your heart, body, mind and soul.

Progression

We are here to remind you that you are strong! Stay positive because every step brings you one step closer to your goals! No matter how slow you feel like you are going, remember that you are moving. Every step counts!

Know that it is okay to stop, take a break and do *'nothing'*, but if you get back up you are progressing! A little progress each day adds up to big results. Love the *'work in progress'* that is you!

If you feel like you are drifting, ground yourself and clear your mind so that your heart can communicate to you. Go for a walk, open some windows and allow the fresh air to rejuvenate your mind, body and soul. A clear mind leads to a merry heart!

When change occurs, do not resist it. Resisting change is resisting your growth and we want to see you progress and grow on your journey! You cannot become or do what you want if you remain where you are. See any challenges as an opportunity to progress and grow to a heightened state of wellbeing.

Your life does not improve by chance, it improves by change! Change can be difficult and chaotic, but in the end it will be beautiful and inspiring to yourself and others. Keep on going, you have got this!

Another page is calling you…
1.Choose a number you feel drawn to 1,2,3 or 4
2.Move forwards that number of pages

New Beginnings

We want you to remain patient. You are soon to be offered a new beginning, opportunity or fresh start.

No matter how old you are, you are still capable of starting new ventures and trying new experiences. Remember that sometimes some things must come to an end for a new doorway of opportunity to open. Let go of anything that no longer serves you or adds any benefit to your life and embrace what is to come.

You will experience new feelings and emotions when you begin this new chapter in your life. It may take time to adapt to, but embrace this new change with patience and trust!

We will send people to support and guide you through this transition, so be aware and mindful of the wisdom that they bring you. Wisdom is a beautiful thing as you can draw upon different aspects of other people's lives. This is a beautiful gift!

Have faith in your dreams and do not let anyone infiltrate their negativity into your field of happiness. Embrace and accept your own individuality and strengths. This is your time to shine and be who you want to be!

Change

Change is on the horizon and it is to be embraced! Know that this change will benefit you in the long term, even if it feels like an uphill battle.

If you feel like you are struggling, we will send you a direct message of 555 or 5555 on your path. This is a reminder from us that this change is here to benefit your soul! Keep the faith!

We want you to be open to change, starting with yourself. Change occurs in stages within the mind. When you alter your thoughts, it adds more depth at each phase. The result will be the beautiful transformation of yourself and all that you desire from what you have created in your mind.

Know that you cannot change other people, but you can change your behaviour, attitude and actions. If you want a different result, try making a different choice for change to occur. Regardless of what happens, your choice will always serve to benefit you in the long run.

Sometimes your life needs to be turned upside down, shaken and changed to relocate you to the exact place you need to be. Everything happens for a reason. Trust the process; we have got your back!

Self-Maintenance

It is easy to get wrapped up in the hustle and bustle of life, but it is important that you remember to take the time to stop and care for your mental, spiritual and physical wellbeing.

Make a conscious effort to introduce small habitual changes, focusing on self-maintenance. Give yourself time to relax, rest, take a break or have fun to enable your body to flow in its natural rhythmic state.

Indulge in things that make you feel good and increase your energy. When your mind, body and soul are nurtured, those things that cause you stress or worry are less likely to penetrate your energetic field.

Fill yourself up with self-love and care. Self-maintenance will help you re-energise and aid any healing that is needed.

When you give love and light to yourself, it will come back to you like a boomerang in other areas of your life. Love is the most powerful energy that can propel you forward and heal anything!

Family

We want you to know that families are like branches on a tree; they grow in different directions but their roots remain as one. Even when you lose people you love, they always remain within your roots. Whenever you miss them, spend time outdoors near a tree to help you reconnect with them and yourself.

Ensure that you are doing what makes you happy, rather than striving to serve and do things for others. This will only burn you out and lower your vibration because you are not in alignment with your true authentic self.

Taking care of yourself is extremely important, as it contributes to your ability in taking care of others. You are the root of your family but you need to be grounded for it to flourish. Remember that family is not always defined by blood, sometimes it's defined by love.

Spend time grounding and connecting to nature and doing what helps you grow. If that means temporarily disengaging, then go with the flow and let it be.

You are your own unique self and you have your own unique branch. Know that it is ok to outgrow what you once were doing and change direction. This is your life so do not be afraid to live it your way and reach the heights that you dream of!

Healing

Your health is of great importance to us and we want you to function in its full capacity. We love and care about you but we need you to do the same too!

Commit to yourself by maintaining your physical, emotional, psychological and spiritual needs. Eat foods that nourish your body and indulge in healthy habits.

Be present and surround yourself in high vibrational environments such as listening to uplifting, empowering music or affirming strong, inspiring, daily mantras to elevate your emotional and psychological state of mind.

Heal in the presence of nature; listen to uplifting or serene music, soak in a salt bath, exercise, treat yourself, practice daily gratitude, read self-help books, practice mindfulness, meditation, prayer, yoga and Pilates.

If you feel like you are overthinking and struggling to tame your thoughts, try taking time to practise any of the above. This will enable space for enriching things to attract to you. When you are at peace with yourself, happiness will follow and this will aid the healing process.

Transition

If you are going through any changes or disruptions in your health, finances or relationships, rest assured that this situation is only temporary.

It is now time for you to transition into a new area of your life. You need to remain grounded and make yourself adaptable to coping with this change.

Sometimes transition happens when you least expect it so be prepared!

Know that transitioning is a continuous process, which enables you to progress and grow, and start fresh chapters in your book of life.

You will find that, in these transitioning periods, you will shed parts of yourself. You will notice that your circle of friends may change but rest assured that this is all part of the transition and the ebb and flow of life.

It is when you are in a transitional period that you start to come alive, breaking the barriers that once constrained you. From a cocoon that was in a dark place, you then become the beautiful butterfly that is ready to soar to new heights! Remember that change can be good too.

Motivation

A wealth of infinite abundance will be yours if you are motivated enough to attain it. The biggest source of motivation is in your thoughts. Train your mind to keep trying, not allowing thoughts of failure to tie you down.

Fearing failure can essentially cancel out your motivational streak. When you feed fear with more fear, it thrives on this environment to survive. Instead, have no limits and make no excuses, otherwise fear will continue to breed. You can do anything if you completely immerse your mind, body, heart and soul into it, with passion and love!

If you get knocked down, what motivates you to get back up?

Whatever this is, you can use it to push yourself every day because no one else is going to do it for you. This does not mean you need to overexert yourself. Small steps are okay too, there is no rush.

Spend time reflecting and planning what you need to do first and this will help you be more efficient and will save you time in the long run. The time and dedication you pour into what you are doing or intend to do, will produce an overpour of abundance.

So put your motivation pants on and get moving!

Wellbeing

We are worried about your well-being and we want you to know that you can heal yourself by raising your vibration.

Spend time investing in your personal well-being and do what makes you feel happy. Happiness begins with you, not with your relationships, friends or job. You are your own healer and the medicines you need can be found within the energy around and inside of you. Spend less time seeking to please others and focus more on pleasing yourself.

We want you to know that laughing is the antidote to the situation you are currently in. Laughter can help wash away the problems that you face. Laughter is love, light and healing! When you raise the vibrations of your thoughts and feelings, healing naturally takes place.

Take some time away from the normal busy routine of life so you can focus on your own needs. Detox your body and mind and allow positive energies to surge through you, releasing any negative thoughts from your energy field.

We urge you to take a short break, open some windows or go for a walk and revitalise your body with fresh air.

Protection

Have courage to stand firm and hold your space in order to protect your energy field. Be aware that holding onto pride, resentment or anger can potentially prevent you from expanding. Holding onto these qualities is like holding onto a hot piece of coal with the intention of throwing it at someone else, but the only person who will get burnt is you!

In order to prevent you from absorbing negativity, getting hurt or lowering your energy and vibration, release anything that does not serve you.

Shield and protect yourself by visualising a pure white bubble of love and light around you, especially when in toxic environments or when you are feeling depleted. We are always here to protect you and give you an extra shield of protection when you call upon us in this way!

Know that love can penetrate the field of negativity and darkness in your life, but remember that darkness CANNOT penetrate love and light!

You are a Warrior of Light and here for a divine purpose! Have faith that you can withstand any storm. Visualise yourself with an armour of love placed upon you, so you are ready to enter any situation that you may face with courage and valour!

Relationships

We want you to allow faith to be the driving force to receive abundance in your work or relationships. Let go of any financial or relationship worries that you currently hold. Have faith that we will see you through this situation.

Know that we are diligently watching you throughout this process. The stronger your faith, the stronger the relationship becomes and the stronger you magnetise what you want into your life.

Know that good relationships do not just happen overnight; they take time, commitment, perseverance, love and patience. Build upon these daily with those around you and life will become more balanced.

We want you to know that you are never alone, even at times when you feel like you are. If your heart needs companionship, seek friendship and guidance in us and other people who love you like friends or family, but most importantly yourself!

We love you and want to give you the love you require. Commit to what matters the most but know that you are a priority. For relationships to manifest or prosper, you need to maintain your own needs first.

Focus

Have faith in our capability to lead you to abundance. All that you need is available to you, but you must learn to focus your mind and express your intentions clearly to us.

Spending time focusing on your own individual needs is imperative on your journey. Where focus goes, energy flows! Ensure that you are pouring all the love and energy into yourself first.

Starve your distractions and feed your focus by using mindfulness techniques and incorporating them into your daily life. A clear mind helps you to directly focus on the road ahead.

Practise inhaling abundance into your life and exhaling all negative thoughts and feelings. Only then will the areas of love, work and relationships begin to prosper.

Give gratitude to everything in your life and your circuit will flow in a synchronistic and harmonious state.

Stay focused on whatever you want to do, not allowing self-doubt to hold your mind and heart captive! Whenever you find yourself doubting how far you can go, just remember how far you have come!

Take a Chance

We send this message for you to consider taking a chance on changing what you are currently doing and to release your inner self from the walls that you have surrounded it with.

Do not allow your soul to be locked away because you fear taking a chance on something. If you allow fear to drive your decisions, you could miss out on all the wonderful things that life has to offer you!

You can overcome those hurdles you fear by rising above them and acting now. If you try but fail, get back up and try again! There are so many opportunities calling out to you, but you need to take a chance and take that leap of faith!

See life as an adventure by having fun and living in the present moment of now. Contemplate doing something new that pushes you beyond what you '*think*' is your sanctuary. Your sanctuary is your state of mind, not your environment! It can be found in places where you are happy and experience a state of bliss! This will help you on your journey.

We want you to create space to play more and work less. Trust your soul's guidance and you will experience greater freedom.

Love & Commitment

Self-love is an ocean and your heart is a vessel. Commitment into self-care will produce an over pour of love both for yourself and humanity!

This is a divine time to concentrate and put the love and commitment into what sets your soul on fire! The things that bring you joy make you happy, and when you are happy, abundance follows! You can then inject this into your work, relationships, goals or dreams.

Aim to keep your intentions and actions balanced and in unity. Take more time to balance your work, family and social life. When you have balance, everything else will begin to fall into place. If you act with love, you will receive acts of love in return.

Love is patient; quality time needs to be invested in yourself so that you can function better. If you decide to commit to something, make sure you invest the right amount of time and effort to fulfil this. Remember, love and commitment are acts not words.

Stay motivated and continuously remind yourself that YOU have the power to create the life you want, but you must invest in yourself with happiness and love first!

Purpose

Know that everyone discovers their soul purpose at different stages of their lives and this is orchestrated divinely! If you know your soul purpose, do not lose sight of it. Know that every 'bad' day serves a purpose and aids you in your progression.

If you do not know or fully understand your soul purpose yet, do not worry. Everything will unfold as and when it should. Everything happens when it is intended; trust the process and keep moving forwards.

Know that your path is not always a straight line sometimes there are twists and turns along the way. If you go down the *'wrong'* road and you get *'lost'*, do not worry. You may think you are lost, but you could be exactly where you need to be and perhaps about to discover something significant to aid you on your journey in the future. Remember, everything happens for a reason!

The experiences you have endured so far have taught you valuable lessons to help you grow. Your strength arises from the continuous efforts and struggles that you have overcome. We have watched and supported you throughout these times and we are proud of your achievements.

11:11 Wakeup Call

You are in the supreme powerhouse of 1111 and this is our 11:11 wakeup call to you! Yes, if you have not already, it is time to wake up, pay attention and follow your heart's calling.

Your journey to find or lead your true-life purpose is upon you. You opened this page because we are nudging you to wake up and shift to where your heart and dreams yearn to go.

Set your intentions and feed them with positive thoughts. Recognize that your words, thoughts, and feelings contain great power. Utilise them to benefit you by nurturing your mind like a garden, pulling out the weeds that have the capability to take over. Water yourself daily with love and remove what does not serve you. Only then will you grow as the beautiful soul you were designed to be.

You are here for a much grander purpose. You are a warrior of love and light who can aid humanity in so many ways never forget that! When you see 11:11 or 1111 know that you are never alone and that you are guided by us always.

Youthfulness

It does not matter how old you are in years, what matters is the youthfulness of your character and inner self!

Do not allow your body, mind and spirit to be limited by your age. You are still young at heart and your time here is still to be enjoyed and relished.

As time goes on, what you enjoy and appreciate continuously changes. You may have enjoyed being more physically adventurous when you were younger, but you now prefer peaceful walks or staying at home. And that is okay. It does not mean you are '*old*', it simply means that your palate has changed.

The real fountain of youth is to have a pure heart and lead from your authentic self! It is your mind, talents and creativity that you bring to the table that changes the dynamics of life.

Know that whatever your age, there's always room for dreams and ambitions or to develop yourself and the world around you. Never give up or allow time to stop you!

Adventure

We want you to step out of your comfort zone and be spontaneous because this is the best kind of adventure your soul needs! The best moments happen when they are unplanned, random and spontaneous.

If you are too busy working or trying to fit in with the rest of society, how will you ever know how amazing you could be or the amazing things you could do or experience? If you are constantly surrounded by people absorbing your energy and you are feeling depleted, go take yourself on an adventure. Happiness, love and adventure are all within your reach!

We can hear your inner child screaming out to be released and we want to see you slow down. Do not worry or rush things, instead honour your inner child by losing yourself in life's simple pleasures!

Now is the perfect time to loosen up and shake that rigidity and routine away. When you begin to loosen up, you will notice other people around you loosen up too. Sometimes the most productive thing you can do is relax.

Life is a beautiful adventure! Surround yourself with beautiful people, things or places. Live your best life and live every moment of it because you only get one chance to do it!

Reassurance

We can help you restore anything you need and change it into something amazing. All you need is faith in us and yourself! Do not let one *'bad'* day or situation make you feel like you are enduring a bad life.

We walk beside you and hold you up in your time of need. We are gently guiding you on your path, but you need to work with us to help you heal or move forward. Have trust and faith that we will answer your calls.

We surround you with love and light, giving you gentle nudges through signs and synchronicities. Be open to receiving these by paying attention and being more aware of who and what surrounds you.

If you see feathers, know that we are offering you comfort and reassurance and know that you are not alone! This is also a sign that your loved ones who have transitioned are also with you, giving their support to you during this time.

We envelope you with a warm loving hug and embrace you tightly. Feel this love and use it to help you get back up!

Change Your Thoughts

Your life is a mere reflection of what you think. If you change your thoughts, you change your life. Work to balance the union of your mind with faith.

The joy that can enter your life is limitless. Joy, love, happiness and abundance is dependent upon the quality of your thoughts.

The more grateful you are for what you have, the better you will feel and the quicker your manifestations will appear.

Balance your thoughts with positivity and then tip the scales so your mindset is elevated above the negative events and people that infiltrate your life.

Let positivity dominate and take the central stage in your mind. It is time to serve an eviction notice to the negative committee that resides in your mind and get positive tenants to thrive inside! A happy mind is a happy home!

Time Management

We feel that now is the time for some quiet reflection. When you know how to silence what distracts you, it is then that you become more aware of where and how you can better use your time.

Stop saying: *'I don't have time to do things'* or *'there's not enough time in the day'*, as you are only creating obstacles for yourself! Consider where you can adjust things to create more time. It is up to you to invest your time into what is important to you. No one else is responsible for this but you.

Write down what you need to do and organise a structured plan of how and when you will do this. You can then effectively manage your own time and expectations, as well as others.

It is important to include time for yourself and your loved ones. When you balance your time with the needs of yourself, you become more focused and ready to face each day.

Grounding

We know that you want to feel free and fly high in everything you do but we want you to know that in order to fly, you must start from the ground. The more grounded you are, the higher you will fly.

It is through practise, patience and perseverance that you will begin to navigate through any storms you may face on your path. If you are feeling all over the place, use some of these grounding techniques to help you:

-Walk barefooted, connecting with mother nature.
-Hug a tree or meditate underneath one.
-Visualise yourself either under a tree connecting to the roots or even better, be the tree!
-Wade in water, fill your lungs with fresh air by going for a walk or opening your windows.

Raise your face to the warmth of the sun and connect with the fire. Raise your face to the bright, shining moon and connect with the light. It is then that you will feel and absorb the vast power and energy within your very being!

Nature does not just ground you, it also nourishes, heals and transforms you. It helps you to grow and blossom into the beautiful being you were designed to be!

Warrior Spirit

It takes great force to face other people's opinions and criticisms, but you can overcome this. We know that you have done it before and we want you to know that you can do it again! When you can silence other people's voices from your mind, your own voice can prevail!

This is your life and nobody else's, so take the reins and control it by releasing the warrior spirit within you! Be courageous and assertive in any decisions that you make. Rather than thinking about what you cannot do, focus your thoughts and attention on what you can and will do!

You are standing with an army of Angels beside you, you can do anything! There is no need to lower your expectations to fit in. You are perfect just as you are! We want you to know that you were born to shine, so never let anyone dim your beautiful sparkle.

Everything you need is already inside you! That is the secret people do not tell you. When you feel like giving up, we are the voice of hope that whispers, *"try again!"*

Your warrior spirit will always succeed because you were born with it!

Overcoming Challenges

Rather than looking at problems as obstacles, see them as challenges that you can overcome. Unfortunately, being challenged in life is inevitable, but succumbing to it is optional. You have the choice to bulldoze through any challenges that you meet.

We understand that life can often feel difficult with these challenges that you face but have faith that you will reap the rewards if you continue to persevere and overcome your trials and tribulations.

Know that you have the strength that is needed to overcome every hurdle and adversity that you face. When you challenge yourself, you will realise the true potential of who you can become or what you can do!

Visualise yourself as a tree, keeping your roots grounded and you will be able to weather any storm. Remember that after every storm follows a rainbow!

Stand strong and have courage as your companion to guide your way. Keep the faith and know that the situation you are in will soon subside. We are working behind the scenes to help you. Trust in us as we trust in you!

1111 Pay Attention

We are your Angelic team and you were drawn to this page because we are nudging you in order to get your attention. Pay attention to the signs, synchronicities and people that we bestow upon you on your journey are rare treasures in disguise. Do not allow your judgements to intervene, as this would be unfavourable to our intended outcome for you.

When you see 11:11 or 1111, this is us reminding you to stop for a moment and become more aware of your surroundings, thoughts and feelings. Look around and observe everything that you can see, hear, feel or sense. These messages we send can be embedded within songs, numbers, repeated words or advertisements that you see or hear.

Sometimes the things that you believe to be minor, are more important than you think. When you really pay attention, you will see that everything around you is guiding you!

Change in Direction

We have watched you push yourself either mentally, emotionally or physically. We want you to stop, think and reflect on specific areas in your life that are causing you stress or disharmony.

Take time to focus and reflect on what you have been doing and see where adjustments can be made to help construct the change that is required to reach your destination, even if that means a change of destination. This does not make you a failure; it is about what makes you happy!

If you have a passion, creative idea or project, now is the time to start or finish it. The seeds that you plant with love, hard-work and dedication will bloom and produce a fruitful life for you.

If you want different or better results, think about making different choices! A change in direction could be just what you need to restore the balance in your life.

Adventure

We want you to step out of your comfort zone and be spontaneous because this is the best kind of adventure your soul needs! The best moments happen when they are unplanned, random and spontaneous.

If you are too busy working or trying to fit in with the rest of society, how will you ever know how amazing you could be or the amazing things you could do or experience? If you are constantly surrounded by people absorbing your energy and you are feeling depleted, go take yourself on an adventure. Happiness, love and adventure are all within your reach!

We can hear your inner child screaming out to be released and we want to see you slow down. Do not worry or rush things, instead honour your inner child by losing yourself in life's simple pleasures!

Now is the perfect time to loosen up and shake that rigidity and routine away. When you begin to loosen up, you will notice other people around you loosen up too. Sometimes the most productive thing you can do is relax.

Life is a beautiful adventure! Surround yourself with beautiful people, things or places. Live your best life and live every moment of it because you only get one chance to do it!

Move with Love

Love is the driver that steers you towards your destination. You cannot move without it. It will benefit you if you let go of any resentment or anger you hold onto, because it will only prevent you from moving forward diligently.

If you feel like your emotions are taking control of you, spend time meditating or praying, clearing your mind from distractions so you can receive the guidance you need.

Make a conscious effort to spend more time with those you love and be grateful for what you have and how you received it. In order to build on your relationships, commitment is required by investing time and love into them. But first you need to pour love into yourself. This is not essential, it is necessary!

The source of your actions should always come from a place of love. Work hard on giving love daily to yourself then to those around you and the work you do.

Spend time doing something that satisfies your soul. Time invested in self-care and love will rejuvenate and re-energise you, so that you can focus on the outcome you want to receive.

1111 Pay Attention

We are your Angelic team and you were drawn to this page because we are nudging you in order to get your attention. Pay attention to the signs, synchronicities and people that we bestow upon you on your journey are rare treasures in disguise. Do not allow your judgements to intervene, as this would be unfavourable to our intended outcome for you.

When you see 11:11 or 1111, this is us reminding you to stop for a moment and become more aware of your surroundings, thoughts and feelings. Look around and observe everything that you can see, hear, feel or sense. These messages we send can be embedded within songs, numbers, repeated words or advertisements that you see or hear.

Sometimes the things that you believe to be minor, are more important than you think. When you really pay attention, you will see that everything around you is guiding you!

Realign

We want you to know that grounding is essential right now! The energy within your body is like a wheel that is spinning and rotating. We can see that you currently have blockages within this energetic wheel, and we want to help you realign them.

Make sure you are grounding daily by connecting with nature, meditating, holding grounding stones or crystals. Seek out energetical healers to aid the restoration process. Even healers need healing!

Do not lose sight of your purpose by allowing your negative experiences from the past or present pull you down. This will only interfere with your vibration and energetic field.

Know that any challenges you face are happening for a purpose and when you accept this, you will start to grow.

We want you to know that you are a lightworker here to help others learn and grow from your own experiences. That is why you are a warrior of light! You can help them overcome the fears they face and show them a different perspective. However, before you do this, you need to have the energy and capacity within yourself to act upon this.

You have a significant influence on the destinies of many others and it is therefore vital that you are perfectly aligned.

Assertiveness

This reading serves as a reminder to be more assertive when you need to be. Know that it is okay to say *"no"* sometimes. Why say yes to things at the cost of your own happiness?

It is time to concentrate on yourself, to do what needs to be done to move forward and reach your intended destination. You need to focus on thinking about your own needs more and not putting other people's needs first. Having the courage to be honest and open with other people and yourself is essential for your progression.

Getting caught up worrying about other people's opinions or beliefs will not always benefit your progression. Be aware of external factors that may affect any decisions that you make. Allowing or absorbing what others dictate to you will not serve you in the long-term.

Instead, rely on your own expertise and knowledge and apply what you know or feel to the situation, instead of asking for someone else's opinion.

Talk to yourself sometimes, when you need expert advice!

You Can Do It!

We want you to know that you can do anything when you put your mind, body, heart and soul into it. You are a powerful being of love and light. Lead your life as a positive example to others. If you fall, get back up! You are a warrior!

People around you may criticise or doubt what you say or do, but you can use this as fuel to propel you forward and show them what you are really made of!

Know that you CAN do anything. Anything is possible if you conceive it in your mind first! If you are offered support from people around you, do not be proud or dismiss them. You have the choice to let go of pride, anger or resentment and accept the help that is offered to you if it resonates. This is us supporting and guiding you in your times of need, orchestrating the people to be in the right place at the right time for you.

If there is a new job, project or idea that you feel passionate about, put those thoughts into action. If you have already started something and have not finished it, get it back out and start *operation revival!*

Actions are what get the ball rolling. Nothing will move or change otherwise!

Independence

This page serves as a reminder for you to take a break to reflect and regain the strength for you to independently move forward in the current situation you are in.

Know that you are not alone and your loved ones you miss are always present within your beautiful heart. Remember that after every storm, a rainbow follows. When you see a rainbow, know that this is a sign from a loved one giving you a message; to have courage and to remind you of your strength!

We urge you to spend time with yourself. Solitude is a place where your mind increases in strength and learns to lean upon itself. Your mind then becomes self-sufficient and you no longer need to rely on the advice or opinions of others. When you look within, all the answers will surface. This will guide you to your destination and bring happiness into your life.

You have the power to construct the life that you want. Do not be afraid to speak up for yourself or say 'no' when you do not want to do something. You are much more powerful than you think. Now, trust your power and believe in yourself. It is your independence that will give you the wings to fly!

Opportunities

In order to make space for new opportunities, it's essential to abandon what does not aid you in your transformation. Everything you think, feel and believe, you attract into your energetical field. We want you to be aware of your thoughts and actions because every action has an equal reaction.

Focus upon what it is that you want, but do not worry about how or when this will come to you. Believe that you have the power to manifest anything you want, and we will orchestrate the opportunities for you.

Have trust and faith that we are working in your favour to help you fulfil what it is that you need and desire. Pay attention to the signs that we send you, you may not notice them if your mind is working in overdrive!

By practising gratitude daily, you will draw everything you need like a magnet. This is when doors of opportunities will present themselves to you unexpectedly. Remember that the power of the mind is the key to your success. Gratitude is the vitamin for your soul and the vital component to opening the doors of abundance and opportunities into your life.

Trust the process and remain patient there is a plan in place for your beautiful Soul!

Service

You will notice that others around you will become more drawn to you to seek your help and guidance. Use your experiences and inner wisdom to help them. The tools you have are all within you, trust in your instincts to guide your words.

Always remember that helping others also helps yourself because you rise when you lift others up, consequently shifting your energy to vibrate on a higher level. When you lose yourself in the service of others, you will discover your own happiness and understand what makes your own light shine brighter.

Be aware of your boundaries and learn to recognise when your energy starts to become too depleted. It is good to help others but make sure you find the right balance. Remember to always look after yourself too.

You cannot give to others if you have not given to yourself first. Feed yourself with an abundance of self-love and care and declutter what does not serve you.

We are a divine source and we are always here to help you, should you need any guidance. Just call upon us and we will always answer your call.

Individuality

We want you to know that you are a precious gift to the world and here for a great purpose. You are a unique individual and that is your superpower!

You are enough and there is no need for you to imitate or copy what others are doing. Whether you realise it yet or not, you are here in this world to be an original, not a copy! Remember to be led by your true authentic self because this is what makes you stand in your superpower of individuality.

You are a beacon of light and can reach people in dark places. If you ever feel like you are in a dark place or feel vulnerable, fill yourself up with self-love and care. Most importantly, be kind to yourself.

Know that your vulnerability is a beautiful attribute because you are having the courage to be seen for the authentic individual you are. Vulnerability is your greatest measure of courage. Remember that courage does not mean you do not get scared, it means you do not allow fear to stop you!

Step outside of your comfort zone and the box that society has put you in, regain your power and shine your own beautiful light. Be the unique individual you were designed to be!

Self-Care

If you are depleted, low or emotional, self-care is required before you burn out! This is our warning to you. Listen to your body when you need to rest and rejuvenate. If you do not have energy, you will struggle to carry out the work that needs to be done.

We see that it is time to fuel yourself up by pampering the needs of your body so your mind can relax, and your heart can slow down.

Support yourself by maintaining and nourishing your mind, body, spirit, and soul. It is important to give yourself permission to take a break and enjoy life!

Applying self-care into your life will make you more efficient and productive, creating an opening for change to enter. When you make space for yourself and declutter, you will be able to hold a space to help others too.

You will find that this brings you great pleasure, satisfaction, and fulfilment. This cathartic feeling is both soothing and healing. Remember, life is for making, but do not forget to look after yourself as this is vital for your development and growth!

Reassurance

We can help you restore anything you need and change it into something amazing. All you need is faith in us and yourself! Do not let one '*bad*' day or situation make you feel like you are enduring a bad life.

We walk beside you and hold you up in your time of need. We are gently guiding you on your path, but you need to work with us to help you heal or move forward. Have trust and faith that we will answer your calls.

We surround you with love and light, giving you gentle nudges through signs and synchronicities. Be open to receiving these by paying attention and being more aware of who and what surrounds you.

If you see feathers, know that we are offering you comfort and reassurance and know that you are not alone! This is also a sign that your loved ones who have transitioned are also with you, giving their support to you during this time.

We envelope you with a warm loving hug and embrace you tightly. Feel this love and use it to help you get back up!

Completion

You chose this page because we need to give you a gentle nudge in the right direction!

We are here to remind you to take the steps and actions required to continue moving forward or completing intended goals. Habit, persistence and perseverance is what will see you through to the end.

If you have an idea, start to implement it now, envisioning it in completeness. If you have already started something, continue to execute it to the finish line. Do not expect others to do it for you - the ball is in your court now! It takes focus, determination and practise to aim high in order to succeed.

Achievement, success, desire and dreams are all connected with action. Even if you feel like you will or are making *'mistakes'*, keep moving and do not give up. You can do anything if you shift your mind into positive gear! When you do, you will be cruising in the fast lane in no time!

The best thing you can invest in is YOU! Have faith and courage in your own abilities and see things through to the end.

Play

We have been observing you and we want you to know that more time needs to be made for having fun!

We have noticed your mind and body have been working hard lately and your energy levels could do with a boost! Too much work and not enough play is not good for the mind, body or soul.

You cannot give your energy to other people or projects if you do not have enough reserved for yourself. Therefore, it is essential to take time out for yourself and participate in activities that satisfy your soul and help re-energise your being.

When you spend time in a state of "play", you can release the load that burdens your precious being. Spend time being with or around children and release your inner child that is yearning to be set free!

See, feel and listen to the world from the goodness of your heart. Smile, laugh and bask in the ambience of fun! This will open your senses and give you more clarity and direction in your life.

This is what your body requires to restore your energy. When your energy is restored, you become more effective and efficient in everything that you do.

Disconnect To Reconnect

We want you to be mindful of your current environment. Know that you can walk away from anything that does not serve you or make you happy. This does not always mean just physically walking away, but mentally and emotionally too.

Declutter and disconnect from any negative words or actions, being mindful not to respond, react or retaliate. In these situations, silence is the best remedy. Do not be the one that fuels the fire, as the only person who will get burnt is you. Hold your integrity this is everything!

Have faith that any struggles you are facing at present will soon resolve. Spending time by yourself, reconnecting with mother nature, crystals or listening to meditation music will help you zone out from everything that distracts you. This will also help re-energise you and give you the nudge you need.

To hear yourself and our guidance, you need to be able to disconnect to reconnect again. This can only be done if you unplug the undesirable thoughts and people that pollute your mind! When you feel more grounded you can re-plug yourself into the world because you have rebooted your system to full optimism!

Slow Down

We urge you to think before making any big decisions at this moment in time. It does not benefit you to continue your daily life in a rushed, tired or stressed state, and we therefore need you to take a moment to breathe and slow down.

It is important for you to understand that rushing things can often result in a less qualitative outcome. Slow down, regain your strength and then get back on the road with a patient, calm, clear mind. You will still reach the same goal, but you will feel a lot lighter carrying less stress along the way!

Try and do things that give you a sense of enjoyment and fulfilment and allow any stress or tension that you have been harbouring to gently ease away.

We ask you to be more mindful and aware when you need to give love to your body and mind. Know when enough is enough and when you need to stop! If your body and mind are feeling tired, exhausted or depleted, this is a sign that you need to take a break, relax, refresh and re-energise.

Remember, life is a journey not a race!

Direction

We feel that there is a deep need for you to contemplate the route you want to travel along, letting your heart navigate you.

We want you to recognise that direction is more important than the speed you are travelling at. You hold the key to your vehicle in your heart and mind, but first you must have faith and trust in the route you envision. If you can see it, feel it and believe it, the path ahead will become much clearer.

At points on your journey you will need to rely on your own intuition and independence. If travelling alone makes you feel fearful or anxious, know that the journey you face unaccompanied can also make you the strongest! Remember, walking alone is sometimes better than walking with people who do not value you!

Remember, you are in control of the steering wheel. You decide which direction you want to go in!

Have faith that the journey you are on is destined for you and has a purpose, however tough it may seem. Know that there are no bad decisions, as there are always lessons to be learnt from every situation. Keep moving, one foot in front of the other. Small steps are better than no steps!

Organisation

We want you to invest in your time wisely. Organisation will help in shortening the road to your goals and dreams and reduce stress and clutter in the process. This will save you time and money, thus giving you a better quality of life and more freedom to grow and move in different directions.

Remember that organising or cleaning is a practise. Stay on top of it, being mindful not to get complacent because this will only deplete your time and energy further down the line. Being organised requires discipline; if you practice this every day it will become a habit that will aid you in your everyday life.

When you organise your environment and mind, you release all the clutter that does not serve you. This disarray, chaos and imbalance affects your energy and can block you from moving forward on the path of abundance and opportunities.

Organisation enables you to manage and take control of your life and have clarity in all that you see and do. Remember that a tidy space is a tidy mind!

Music

If you are feeling low or you are struggling to focus, listen to high frequency sounds or music to help stimulate you and heighten your energy to vibrate on a higher level.

Remember that music and sounds can rapidly affect your mood and alter your vibrational frequency. Listen to music that makes you feel empowered, inspired, motivated and uplifted. Singing also helps you feel the vibrations more powerfully within your body.

Music has the power to change your world and the world of others around you, if you learn to feel rather than just hear.

If you are struggling to sleep at night, try and meditate with calm, relaxing music to ease your mind and soothe you to sleep. Through music, meditation and sleep, your body will be able to heal and recover from any stresses that have been troubling you.

Remember that we always send you signs and messages in the music that you listen to or hear around you. Pay attention!

Lightworker

You are a lightworker and here for a greater purpose. We are aware that you are at your happiest when you are helping others.

People are drawn to your veracious energy and the light that you radiate. Be aware of your own energy supply and ensure you are not depleting when offering help and advice to those who need it. With your highly attuned empathic abilities, it is quite easy to absorb their emotions or negativity to drain your own energy. It is vital that you learn to ground and protect your auric field!

In order to help make the world a better place and awaken others to the true beauty of life, it is essential to lead the way by example. Listen to your body and soul when you are feeling tired or low, this is a sign that your energy is depleted.

It is necessary to take time to rest and recharge your batteries and close yourself off temporarily for spiritual maintenance. You can only give and serve others if you are in a place where your own cup is overflowing.

Pay attention when you see lights flickering. This is a sign that we are with you and a reminder that you are guided and protected by the light. Your energy is a beautiful and powerful force. You have the power and gifts to raise the collective consciousness and shift humanity to another dimension!

Independence

This page serves as a reminder for you to take a break to reflect and regain the strength for you to independently move forward in the current situation you are in.

Know that you are not alone and your loved ones you miss are always present within your beautiful heart. Remember that after every storm, a rainbow follows. When you see a rainbow, know that this is a sign from a loved one giving you a message; to have courage and to remind you of your strength!

We urge you to spend time with yourself. Solitude is a place where your mind increases in strength and learns to lean upon itself. Your mind then becomes self-sufficient and you no longer need to rely on the advice or opinions of others. When you look within, all the answers will surface. This will guide you to your destination and bring happiness into your life.

You have the power to construct the life that you want. Do not be afraid to speak up for yourself or say 'no' when you do not want to do something. You are much more powerful than you think. Now, trust your power and believe in yourself. It is your independence that will give you the wings to fly!

Inner Child

It is time to awaken and reconnect with your inner child again. This is where your true authentic self resides. It is the original piece of you that is pure, innocent and connected to your heart. Honour your inner child by living in the present moment of now. When you lose yourself in simple pleasures, you recognise how much there is to love about life.

This is how young children live and they are the most precious gifts in the world. It is now time to unleash your inner child as it wants to come out and play!

Spend time in the company of young children and observe their world through their eyes. Ask questions, get involved and perhaps you will see and feel the magic in everything too!

You may be growing on your journey and in age, but you can still stay young at heart if you unleash your inner child.

Remember when you were young, wild, curious and full of life and energy. Do not let life tame that beautiful authentic side. Embrace your inner child and you will experience a tremendous amount of love and healing. This is needed for your soul to thrive!

Release

We have noticed that you have been holding onto things, which are suppressing your true authentic self. You must heal and restore yourself by releasing any fears or emotions that are blocking you. Resisting this process will only deter you from your path. You have the strength to face anything!

You may feel that a lot of issues you face run in your family, but we are here to guide, empower and reassure you that this pattern does not need to continue with you. You can break the ancestral ties that are preventing you from moving forward.

Know that you can transform pain into power and even empower others from your own personal experiences. This includes any trials, tribulations or harrowing events you have faced.

When you choose not to respond to an emotional impulse such as anger, rage or heartache, you are halfway there! Release any emotional energy and focus on acceptance, as this will help restore the balance.

Know that the past can be painful, but the beautiful thing about it is that it forces you to learn what does not serve or benefit you for your present and future journeys.

Energy

We have noticed that your mind and body have been in constant over-drive. We suggest creating time to relax, take a break or slow down.

Take time to meditate or connect to our divine energy. You have the power to access it whenever you want and to gain a deeper insight. Tap into this energy as it will guide you on your journey.

Life is for enjoying and when you enjoy what you are doing, your energy naturally amplifies. You will then be vibrating on a higher frequency and become much more proficient in what you do.

The energy you emit creates your life. If you are feeling drained or tired, your energy is not functioning as well as it could be. Take some time to stop and recharge in order to heal your soul and receive the optimal energy for you to perform.

Keep your vibrations elevated by ensuring you are looking after your wellbeing. Fill yourself up with self-love, care and worth. This is a necessity for your journey!

High vibrational energy is infectious and has the aptitude to spread ripples far and wide. For what you deliver, you also receive!

Contemplation

If you feel like you have come to a standstill in a specific area of your life or are currently stalling, contemplate on what could be holding you back.

Reflect upon your past and present circumstances and unearth any potential knowledge or expertise that will help you move forward. Remind yourself of the love that is or was once around you. Feel and breathe in the memories and harness that love to move you forward in your situation.

The road you are on may sometimes feel uncertain, but at least you are on a road. You just need to decide which direction you want to go. Trust your intuition for it guides you well.

We want you to know that to achieve anything externally, you must first contemplate changing how you think and feel internally. If you change your focus and let go of what does not serve your highest good, you create space for fulfilment to enter your life. The road ahead then becomes much clearer.

Start each day with gratitude and love. In return you will be blessed with all that you need. When you operate like a magnet, you will attract everything that matches your frequency. Now that is something serious to contemplate on!

Balancing Relationships

We have been watching you and see that there is a deep need for you to balance your desires, goals and dreams with the relationships you have with others.

The labour of work, or what you are currently doing at present, requires a balance of commitment with your relationships with your loved ones. This is the driving force that enables you to succeed in any environment. Love is the pivotal force that catapults you to your destination! If what you are doing is burning you out, spend more time doing things that light you up! This will propel you further in the long-term.

Perhaps consider whether you are committed and working to the best of your ability in what you are doing and in your relationships with others. Are you being present in your relationships or are you too busy working, over-thinking or being consumed by technology?

If you become less distracted by things that are not beneficial to your soul, you will generate more time to invest in the things that you love the most. When you become more present, love, happiness and abundance will certainly arise.

Opportunities

In order to make space for new opportunities, it's essential to abandon what does not aid you in your transformation. Everything you think, feel and believe, you attract into your energetical field. We want you to be aware of your thoughts and actions because every action has an equal reaction.

Focus upon what it is that you want, but do not worry about how or when this will come to you. Believe that you have the power to manifest anything you want, and we will orchestrate the opportunities for you.

Have trust and faith that we are working in your favour to help you fulfil what it is that you need and desire. Pay attention to the signs that we send you, you may not notice them if your mind is working in overdrive!

By practising gratitude daily, you will draw everything you need like a magnet. This is when doors of opportunities will present themselves to you unexpectedly. Remember that the power of the mind is the key to your success. Gratitude is the vitamin for your soul and the vital component to opening the doors of abundance and opportunities into your life.

Trust the process and remain patient there is a plan in place for your beautiful Soul!

Notice the Signs

We want you to slow down so that you can notice the signs we send you. Look out for number sequences, feathers, dimes, robins, hummingbirds, rainbows and ladybirds. These are all signs you are on the right track and that you are being guided by us and any loved ones who have passed away.

We also want you to be aware of what other people are going through. Remember, you notice more when you are silent and observing. Think before you speak or react. This is our wisdom to you.

If you notice any signs of pain, negativity or anger in others, tap into your compassionate nature to help them but make sure you do not absorb their feelings or energy. As an empathic soul, it is crucial that you protect your energy by firmly grounding yourself.

You can also help those who are suffering through prayer, intention or meditation by sending them love and light. This will also help you with your own healing and growth as well as theirs. When you are serving others through the eyes of love and compassion, you receive that love and healing back to yourself as well.

11:11 Wakeup Call

You are in the supreme powerhouse of 1111 and this is our 11:11 wakeup call to you! Yes, if you have not already, it is time to wake up, pay attention and follow your heart's calling.

Your journey to find or lead your true-life purpose is upon you. You opened this page because we are nudging you to wake up and shift to where your heart and dreams yearn to go.

Set your intentions and feed them with positive thoughts. Recognize that your words, thoughts, and feelings contain great power. Utilise them to benefit you by nurturing your mind like a garden, pulling out the weeds that have the capability to take over. Water yourself daily with love and remove what does not serve you. Only then will you grow as the beautiful soul you were designed to be.

You are here for a much grander purpose. You are a warrior of love and light who can aid humanity in so many ways never forget that! When you see 11:11 or 1111 know that you are never alone and that you are guided by us always.

Believe

We would like to see you letting go of anything that is currently worrying you by releasing your feelings to us. Move away from the worry of *'when'* or *'how'* things are going to happen. Instead, start changing your thoughts and believing that they will!

If you believe that you can do it or have it, believe that you deserve it and believe that you'll receive it, you will reach abundance and success in all that you desire.

Having belief will give you the balance you require to move forward diligently. Have faith and believe in yourself, and you will be unstoppable!

Reminding yourself and saying these affirmations daily may be the medicine you need to give you the confidence boost required:

I AM Amazing
I AM Independent
I AM Worthy
I AM Successful

Know your worth, then add tax!

Gratitude

We want you to know that the life you are currently living is like a mirror. It reflects your thoughts, feelings and actions.

Get into a habit of having uplifting thoughts in the morning and before you go to bed. This can change your whole day.

Ingraining daily gratitude into your thoughts each day is important to raise your energy and vibration. The more gratitude you give, the more things you will receive to be grateful for!

Focus on seeing the light at the end of a tunnel when times are a little low or rocky. When you acknowledge all the things that you already have in your life, these acknowledgements will build the foundation for the abundance that you will receive. The more gratitude you express, the stronger that foundation becomes!

Gratitude is a tool that can be used to maintain your physical, mental and spiritual wellbeing. It is the best medicine, for it heals your mind, body and soul. Expressing gratitude, either verbally or written down, is your vitamin for the soul!

Gratitude is like a boomerang; what you throw out into the universe will always come back to you in some shape or form!

Strength

We want you to know that you are not alone. If you are feeling lost, do not give up hope. At times you may feel like others do not understand you and that is okay. There is no need for you to explain or justify the decisions you make or the things that you do. Stand firm with conviction in all that you do, having faith, belief and courage in yourself.

Reflect on a difficult moment in your life that you overcame, then use that experience and the lessons you gained from it to encourage and help you in your present circumstances.

Look deep and find the brave warrior that lies within. Do not accept defeat, you have the power, courage and strength to get through this situation that you are in!

Look in the mirror and see yourself with a vision of love and acceptance. Affirm to yourself your strengths, abilities and skills. By doing this, you will hold space to receive more abundance and love into your life.

The light inside you shines brighter than the darkness around you never forget that!

Believe

We would like to see you letting go of anything that is currently worrying you by releasing your feelings to us. Move away from the worry of *'when'* or *'how'* things are going to happen. Instead, start changing your thoughts and believing that they will!

If you believe that you can do it or have it, believe that you deserve it and believe that you'll receive it, you will reach abundance and success in all that you desire.

Having belief will give you the balance you require to move forward diligently. Have faith and believe in yourself, and you will be unstoppable!

Reminding yourself and saying these affirmations daily may be the medicine you need to give you the confidence boost required:

I AM Amazing
I AM Independent
I AM Worthy
I AM Successful

Know your worth, then add tax!

Self-Care

If you are depleted, low or emotional, self-care is required before you burn out! This is our warning to you. Listen to your body when you need to rest and rejuvenate. If you do not have energy, you will struggle to carry out the work that needs to be done.

We see that it is time to fuel yourself up by pampering the needs of your body so your mind can relax, and your heart can slow down.

Support yourself by maintaining and nourishing your mind, body, spirit, and soul. It is important to give yourself permission to take a break and enjoy life!

Applying self-care into your life will make you more efficient and productive, creating an opening for change to enter. When you make space for yourself and declutter, you will be able to hold a space to help others too.

You will find that this brings you great pleasure, satisfaction, and fulfilment. This cathartic feeling is both soothing and healing. Remember, life is for making, but do not forget to look after yourself as this is vital for your development and growth!

Slow Down

We urge you to think before making any big decisions at this moment in time. It does not benefit you to continue your daily life in a rushed, tired or stressed state, and we therefore need you to take a moment to breathe and slow down.

It is important for you to understand that rushing things can often result in a less qualitative outcome. Slow down, regain your strength and then get back on the road with a patient, calm, clear mind. You will still reach the same goal, but you will feel a lot lighter carrying less stress along the way!

Try and do things that give you a sense of enjoyment and fulfilment and allow any stress or tension that you have been harbouring to gently ease away.

We ask you to be more mindful and aware when you need to give love to your body and mind. Know when enough is enough and when you need to stop! If your body and mind are feeling tired, exhausted or depleted, this is a sign that you need to take a break, relax, refresh and re-energise.

Remember, life is a journey not a race!

Youthfulness

It does not matter how old you are in years, what matters is the youthfulness of your character and inner self!

Do not allow your body, mind and spirit to be limited by your age. You are still young at heart and your time here is still to be enjoyed and relished.

As time goes on, what you enjoy and appreciate continuously changes. You may have enjoyed being more physically adventurous when you were younger, but you now prefer peaceful walks or staying at home. And that is okay. It does not mean you are '*old*', it simply means that your palate has changed.

The real fountain of youth is to have a pure heart and lead from your authentic self! It is your mind, talents and creativity that you bring to the table that changes the dynamics of life.

Know that whatever your age, there's always room for dreams and ambitions or to develop yourself and the world around you. Never give up or allow time to stop you!

Recharge

You were guided to this page because you need to recharge your beautiful soul!

We want you to understand that your life is all about balance. We have noticed that your body and mind have been working in overload and it is time to recharge and restore your energy. We need you to relax, have some respite and take care of yourself.

What you may think is doing *'nothing'*, is actually what brings everything you need into perspective. So, by doing *'nothing'*, you are in fact doing quite a lot! You are resting and recharging. Go with the flow of it opposed to fighting it, otherwise you will burn out fast! You may not see this right now, but we want you to know that this is what is needed!

The question we want to ask you is...

"Do you recharge yourself as much as you recharge your phone?"

Invest in recharging yourself so that you have the power to keep going and moving forward every day.

Pamper yourself with love and attention so that you can prosper. The key to recharging is in self-love and care, which resides in your habits and disciplines. When you wake up every morning, look in the mirror and compliment your radiant being. Recite affirmations to empower the inner Jedi that is screaming to be released!

Moving others

We have seen that you have an inert ability to move people with either your presence, words or touch. You have a magnetic energy that attracts people into your field. Your power to inspire and empower others is moving, motivational and inspiring!

This ability you have to help others also creates a positive energy around you and sends ripples far and wide. You do not always see or hear about how you have impacted others, but we watch and see the beautiful ripples you have created. We want you to stop for a moment and acknowledge all that you are and all that you have done! For this we honour your soul and thank you!

It fills our hearts with joy to know that you can show people how to embrace what they perceive to be '*flaws*' or '*weaknesses*'. Know that the guidance you provide to other people helps them more than you realise, so continue to do what you are doing.

If new people cross your path or old people appear in your life, know that it is for a great purpose. Keep moving with the rhythm of your soul and it will guide you to where it yearns to go. There you will find satisfaction, joy, peace and love.

Believe in Yourself

This message of guidance comes to you because this is an ideal time for you to think about what YOU want, as opposed to what others *'want'* or *'expect'* from you.

You are the captain of your own ship and you can steer it in any direction you wish to sail! Why allow insecurity or fear to prohibit you from cruising out of your comfort zone and travelling into the unknown? We want you to know that this is where your adventure begins. Yes, it is on the other side of fear!

It is fear of the unknown that can often keep you earth bound. You have the choice to allow your soul to grow and soar beyond the limits of restrictive thoughts and feelings.

Believe in yourself and your talents, knowing that there are no limits except the limits you place on yourself.

Have faith in what you do, but above all, have faith in yourself. There is something inside of you that is much greater than any obstacle or challenge. Rise above your deep-rooted fears and ride on the wings of faith and trust. And remember, you are never alone, because we are the wings that you ride on!

Honesty

Honesty is a highly valued and positive quality to possess. Do not expect it but appreciate it when it is freely given.

In relationships, honesty is valued and appreciated and it is where trust is gained. Respect and loyalty can then be given in return. Being honest may not get you many friends, but it will always get you the right ones. It is quality, not quantity that matters!

The power of honesty can be unearthed when you decondition what society has infiltrated in your mind. Do not pretend to be someone you are not in order to impress others or conform to certain expectations.

You should always strive to be your most genuine and authentic self. If you want to experience freedom and happiness, do not hide anything. The greatest advantage of speaking from your authentic self, is that it will flow with ease and you do not have to remember what you said!

Be who you are, not what you think other people want you to be because you will only be travelling your journey as a lie.

Be true to yourself, integrity is everything!

Declutter

If you feel like your life is full of chaos and disharmony, this is a sign that you need to declutter!

Clutter is not just the things in your wardrobe or in the environment around you, it is anything that gets between you and the life that you want to be living. This includes the clutter that resides within your mind too!

Start decluttering your mind and the environment around you. If it does not nourish your soul, get rid of it. It is the unnecessary things that you hold onto that have the aptitude to stunt your growth. If your possessions or thoughts that you hold onto are not serving you, it will not be serving you any better in a box collecting dust or locked up in your mind. Releasing what does not serve you helps your mind and body heal on many levels.

Making space in both your environment and mind allows new opportunities, relationships and ideas to enter your field. When you release the baggage that holds you down, you feel lighter and begin to soar to new heights!

The *"Out with the old and in with the new"* motto springs to our mind! Perhaps you can use this as your affirmation to aid your task of decluttering!

Take a Chance

We send this message for you to consider taking a chance on changing what you are currently doing and to release your inner self from the walls that you have surrounded it with.

Do not allow your soul to be locked away because you fear taking a chance on something. If you allow fear to drive your decisions, you could miss out on all the wonderful things that life has to offer you!

You can overcome those hurdles you fear by rising above them and acting now. If you try but fail, get back up and try again! There are so many opportunities calling out to you, but you need to take a chance and take that leap of faith!

See life as an adventure by having fun and living in the present moment of now. Contemplate doing something new that pushes you beyond what you '*think*' is your sanctuary. Your sanctuary is your state of mind, not your environment! It can be found in places where you are happy and experience a state of bliss! This will help you on your journey.

We want you to create space to play more and work less. Trust your soul's guidance and you will experience greater freedom.

Recharge

You were guided to this page because you need to recharge your beautiful soul!

We want you to understand that your life is all about balance. We have noticed that your body and mind have been working in overload and it is time to recharge and restore your energy. We need you to relax, have some respite and take care of yourself.

What you may think is doing *'nothing'*, is actually what brings everything you need into perspective. So, by doing *'nothing'*, you are in fact doing quite a lot! You are resting and recharging. Go with the flow of it opposed to fighting it, otherwise you will burn out fast! You may not see this right now, but we want you to know that this is what is needed!

The question we want to ask you is…

"Do you recharge yourself as much as you recharge your phone?"

Invest in recharging yourself so that you have the power to keep going and moving forward every day.

Pamper yourself with love and attention so that you can prosper. The key to recharging is in self-love and care, which resides in your habits and disciplines. When you wake up every morning, look in the mirror and compliment your radiant being. Recite affirmations to empower the inner Jedi that is screaming to be released!

Divine Guidance

Our divine light surrounds you with a shield of love and protection. Call upon us for support and guidance to give you the strength and courage you need to put your armour on and overcome any struggles you face.

We want to help you! We have noticed that you have not been grounding yourself enough. Ensuring that you are grounding helps to keep your roots firmly planted on the ground. Strive to spend more time outdoors, allowing the oxygen to revitalize your soul. This will aid your body into adjusting to what is potentially destabilising your alignment. This will assist you in weathering any storm you may face.

Remember who you are and the faculties that you possess. Everything you need to overcome any testing times are stored inside you! Just sprinkle a little faith over the situation and this will aid you in moving forward.

We are your safety net; here to soften the blow and catch you if you fall. Take comfort in the knowledge of this. Trust the process and find the strength, confidence and courage to elevate your soul above the toxicities of life. Above all, keep the faith your story does not end here!

Another page is calling you…
Go either forwards or backwards 3 pages

Actions

Your soul craves to joyfully serve humanity, but you need to be
in an ocean of serenity and bliss to be able to swim and reach
your destination.

The secret to success is when you put your mind, body, heart
and soul into what you do with love and passion.

It is your love and passion that really fuels your actions in
the right direction, which will bring about the change that is
needed. To change and move forward, you must start with
acting on your own needs first!

Once you have invested in yourself, think about your individual
goals and reflect upon what needs to be done to acquire them.
Put your energy and focus wholeheartedly into what it is you
want to achieve.

Know that your actions mould you into who you want
to become, but your words only say who you want to be!
Remember that your actions speak louder than your words.

Plant the seeds you want and then plan on undertaking what
it is you want to accomplish. Keep those thoughts aligned with
only positive thoughts to yield more abundance.

Abundance

We want you to focus on what you have, rather than on what you do not have. Everything you need, you have access to! The wealth of abundance you obtain from within is priceless and extraordinarily limitless!

We know that the situation you have been facing comes from a deep-rooted perception of wealth that has been embedded within you, from a combination of other people, past lives and conditioning. We want to reassure you that money is not to be feared, nor is it the route of all evil! The fear of not having enough money is really an embedded fear that you are not enough. We want you to know that you are enough, and you are all that you need! When you begin to accept this, you will start to detangle and cut the cords of ancestral ties that bind you.

Remember, there is more to life than materialistic possessions.

It is better to be broke with a beautiful heart than rich with intentions that do not serve you! Do what sets your soul on fire by living in the present moment of 'Now' and you will attract all the love and abundance into your life that you require.

Take time each day to express what you are grateful for; from the love that you receive from others, to the air that you breathe that keeps you alive. When you practise this daily, abundance will shift in your favour!

Time

The time that you have is precious and we often see it being wasted. We want you to take the time to reflect upon this...

Ask yourself who and what you are spending your time on? Think about those who might be depleting your time and energy. Consider whether your time might be better served with those that add value to your life.

Heed our words of loving wisdom...

Time costs nothing, but it is valuable and priceless!
You cannot possess it, but you can benefit from it.
You cannot keep time, but you can spend it.
Once you have lost it, you can never get it back!

If you are chasing money for happiness, why not chase happiness and let money flow to you from doing what you love?

Time is not only measured by the hands on a clock but also by your internal rhythm and a collection of your experiences and memories. The reason we urge you to spend your time more wisely is to ensure you continuously experience life in alignment with what benefits you. This keeps your daily rhythm beating on a happy, content note.

Faith in Yourself

See your current situation as a challenge and not as an obstacle. Trust in us and know that a positive outcome is being brought to you. It will align in your favour when the time is right. For now, continue moving forward with faith and remain patient and optimistic.

Know that faith can move mountains but remember, your doubts can create them. If you have lost someone dear to you, know that their presence in your life has given you the tools for you to move forward in difficult times. Reflect upon these and use them to help aid you at this crossroad. Only you can shift the course of your journey through the passage of your actions!

We encourage you to have faith in yourself. Do not ever give up because of one bad chapter in your life. Keep going and do not lose hope. Know that your story does not stop here. Miracles happen just before you are ready to quit!

Be mindful not to compare yourself to others. Learn to feel genuinely happy and content with who you are. Only you can decide who you want to be or what you want to do with the power of your mind and the faith you have in yourself.

We want you to know that you are amazing and you are good enough! Believe in yourself, as we believe in you!

Joy

We love you for who you are and we want to see you filled with joy. We need you to accept yourself for the wonderful person you are and not be ashamed of how others see you.

If you are spending too much time attempting to make others happy, you are only sacrificing your own happiness in the process. Remember that you are only able to give to others that which you have yourself.

If you are not happy, self-care and maintenance need attending to. Always take the time to improve yourself before you start improving other people or things.

Remember that it is important to continuously bring joy into your life and to value yourself. When you are centred in joy, you have the power you need to swiftly move forward. If you are feeling trapped, give your worries to us and we will lift you up.

The key to being happy is knowing that you possess the power to choose what to accept and what to release. Let go of anything that does not serve you because it does not deserve you!

Authentic Self

We want you to find the courage to be authentic. To do this you need to release yourself from everything society and culture has imposed on your beautiful being!

Authenticity is a daily practice of letting go of who you have been conditioned to *think* you are and embracing who you *really* are.

Know that what makes you vulnerable is not a weakness, it is what makes you beautiful, raw and true. Own that vulnerable side that society often labels as a *"weakness"* because we want you to know that it is not! It shows great courage and promotes and facilitates other people to do the same too! As you step into your authentic self, you become a beacon of light to others, helping them feel safe to embrace their true selves.

You are a treasure chest that holds many hidden gems and you are amongst the rarest! When you are living from your authentic self, know that not everyone may like you, but you are growing and transitioning on your path as you should. Be yourself, accept yourself, forgive yourself and value yourself.

When you are in alignment with your true authentic self, abundance and happiness will surge within your remit. You can then bathe in a stream of peace, love and serenity!

Acceptance

We can see that there is a great need for accepting what has happened in the past and releasing everything that is weighing down on your precious wings! Know that nobody's life is *'perfect'*. What you perceive in others as the *'perfect'* life may not be the case behind closed doors! We say this with a wink...
"Never judge a book by its cover."

When you accept that you are perfect just the way you are and that you will always have challenges, you will slowly be able to release the load that is pulling you down.

Learn to recognise that every situation aids your growth. When you do, you will surely flourish! When you place expectations on yourself, relationships or work, you limit the progress of your growth.

Remember that:
'Good people' bring you the gift of love, happiness and memories. Who you consider to be *'bad people'*, bring you the gift of experiences and lessons. Both facets can aid your growth. Every person that crosses your path is therefore a blessing and sometimes in disguise!

Accept everything for the positivity that it can bring and you will lead a positive and abundant life. This is because you will be able to accept things for what they *are* rather than for what you *think* they should be!

Ending of a Situation

You received this message because we want you to know that the ending of a situation and a beginning of a new one is near.

Remember that the relationships around you play an important part in your journey and all serve a purpose. Know that people come and go in your life like the seasons that constantly change. This can bring both pain and joy, but know that it will help both you and them in your growth and progression.

Be aware that it can be difficult to start the next chapter and end any situation you are in if you keep re-reading the last one. Release what is not serving you with love and light, so you can finish what was started, be that in work or a relationship.

Protect your energy and do not allow any negativity or drama to lower your vibration. Instead, turn this negative energy into fuel to succeed in any projects, ideas or work that you are currently undertaking. This is how you can turn pain into power!

When you make any decisions, have faith in the choices you make. Execute this with assertiveness, not allowing other people to doubt your choice. You know what benefits you. Trust your own authority and intuition for it will guide you well.

Confidence

We have watched you successfully overcome so much and we commend you for this!

We believe in you, but we want you to have confidence and belief in yourself too because that is when the magic starts to happen. You will then grow and transition into a beautiful butterfly!

Know that confidence is not about being better than others, it is about having belief in yourself and not comparing yourself to others.

You are a strong individual and we want to reassure you that you have the courage to speak out and do what it is you want. Confidence thrives from leading from your true authentic self and being honest with what you know, say and do.

Declutter what does not serve you so you feel lighter and can move with grace and ease. The most beautiful thing you can wear is a smile! Think of your smile as your armour of confidence even in the bleakest of days and it will help you march on.

You are a beautiful energy of love and light and the world needs to feel your presence. You were born to shine!

Open Your Heart

It is okay to open your heart and let people close to you. Do not allow any previous experiences of pain and suffering become an obstacle in your current relationships.

When you expect love and you are let down, your soul can feel crushed! Fear, anxiety, confusion, pain and disappointment can overwhelm you but If you master the mentality to have no expectations, you will never be disappointed! Finding a place of joy will assist in extinguishing the pain and hurt that you have previously experienced. But to do this, you must first step out of the walls that imprison your heart.

Know that your soul does not always need protecting from love. If you learn to love yourself, you will have all that you need and that will be enough to let your guard down. Always remember that love does not necessarily have to come from others.

Be grateful for everything and everyone already around you and what you possess. But most importantly, look for love within. It is only when you learn to genuinely love yourself and embrace the individual you are that you can put the energy into loving everything and everyone else.

Divine Guidance

Our divine light surrounds you with a shield of love and protection. Call upon us for support and guidance to give you the strength and courage you need to put your armour on and overcome any struggles you face.

We want to help you! We have noticed that you have not been grounding yourself enough. Ensuring that you are grounding helps to keep your roots firmly planted on the ground. Strive to spend more time outdoors, allowing the oxygen to revitalize your soul. This will aid your body into adjusting to what is potentially destabilising your alignment. This will assist you in weathering any storm you may face.

Remember who you are and the faculties that you possess. Everything you need to overcome any testing times are stored inside you! Just sprinkle a little faith over the situation and this will aid you in moving forward.

We are your safety net; here to soften the blow and catch you if you fall. Take comfort in the knowledge of this. Trust the process and find the strength, confidence and courage to elevate your soul above the toxicities of life. Above all, keep the faith your story does not end here!

Another page is calling you...
Choose a page to go to
page 111, 222 or 333

Solitude

Sometimes you need to disconnect from the world to be able to reconnect with yourself and gain more strength. There is nothing more refreshing and rejuvenating than your own company!

Spend time in solitude to connect with your inner self and find the happiness that dwells within. Start a daily gratitude journal to help you reflect upon what makes you feel good every day.

Take a step back from matters that distract you and do not serve you or your purpose. Trust your instincts and do not allow others to influence your decisions or knock your confidence. Be guided by the stillness of your mind, as opposed to other people's chaotic minds.

Have patience in the situation you are in. Gravitate away from overthinking, as this is not healthy for your mind or body and can drown out the sound of your inner voice.

Remember that solitude is not just about silence, it is also about the absence of distraction!

Wellbeing

We are worried about your well-being and we want you to know that you can heal yourself by raising your vibration.

Spend time investing in your personal well-being and do what makes you feel happy. Happiness begins with you, not with your relationships, friends or job. You are your own healer and the medicines you need can be found within the energy around and inside of you. Spend less time seeking to please others and focus more on pleasing yourself.

We want you to know that laughing is the antidote to the situation you are currently in. Laughter can help wash away the problems that you face. Laughter is love, light and healing! When you raise the vibrations of your thoughts and feelings, healing naturally takes place.

Take some time away from the normal busy routine of life so you can focus on your own needs. Detox your body and mind and allow positive energies to surge through you, releasing any negative thoughts from your energy field.

We urge you to take a short break, open some windows or go for a walk and revitalise your body with fresh air.

Solitude

Sometimes you need to disconnect from the world to be able to reconnect with yourself and gain more strength. There is nothing more refreshing and rejuvenating than your own company!

Spend time in solitude to connect with your inner self and find the happiness that dwells within. Start a daily gratitude journal to help you reflect upon what makes you feel good every day.

Take a step back from matters that distract you and do not serve you or your purpose. Trust your instincts and do not allow others to influence your decisions or knock your confidence. Be guided by the stillness of your mind, as opposed to other people's chaotic minds.

Have patience in the situation you are in. Gravitate away from overthinking, as this is not healthy for your mind or body and can drown out the sound of your inner voice.

Remember that solitude is not just about silence, it is also about the absence of distraction!

Change in Direction

We have watched you push yourself either mentally, emotionally or physically. We want you to stop, think and reflect on specific areas in your life that are causing you stress or disharmony.

Take time to focus and reflect on what you have been doing and see where adjustments can be made to help construct the change that is required to reach your destination, even if that means a change of destination. This does not make you a failure; it is about what makes you happy!

If you have a passion, creative idea or project, now is the time to start or finish it. The seeds that you plant with love, hard-work and dedication will bloom and produce a fruitful life for you.

If you want different or better results, think about making different choices! A change in direction could be just what you need to restore the balance in your life.

Another page is calling you…
1.Choose a number you feel drawn to 1,2,3 or 4
2.Move backwards or forwards that number of pages

Honesty

Honesty is a highly valued and positive quality to possess. Do not expect it but appreciate it when it is freely given.

In relationships, honesty is valued and appreciated and it is where trust is gained. Respect and loyalty can then be given in return. Being honest may not get you many friends, but it will always get you the right ones. It is quality, not quantity that matters!

The power of honesty can be unearthed when you decondition what society has infiltrated in your mind. Do not pretend to be someone you are not in order to impress others or conform to certain expectations.

You should always strive to be your most genuine and authentic self. If you want to experience freedom and happiness, do not hide anything. The greatest advantage of speaking from your authentic self, is that it will flow with ease and you do not have to remember what you said!

Be who you are, not what you think other people want you to be because you will only be travelling your journey as a lie.

Be true to yourself, integrity is everything!

Fresh Air

If you feel down, lost or demotivated, take time out to disconnect and recharge your batteries. Open some windows, go for a walk and let the abundance of fresh air revitalize you.

Your mind, body, spirit and soul need some fresh air to heal, rejuvenate and ground your beautiful being! Spend time absorbing yourself in and around nature.

Connect with everything around you; smell, see, feel and hear the beauty in nature that surrounds you. Breathe it into your soul and feel the increase in energy levels. This will open your mind and offer you a fresh perspective.

Spending time in nature is an abundant source of healing that costs you nothing but your time. Investing your time in nature will raise your vibration and is the greatest force for your wellbeing.

You can also switch off from the disturbances of life, toxic situations and people by spending time enjoying your own company. This will give fresh air to your mind because you are silencing the disruptive noise in your head. Sometimes when you disconnect, you reconnect with a stronger signal!

Strength

We want you to know that you are not alone. If you are feeling lost, do not give up hope. At times you may feel like others do not understand you and that is okay. There is no need for you to explain or justify the decisions you make or the things that you do. Stand firm with conviction in all that you do, having faith, belief and courage in yourself.

Reflect on a difficult moment in your life that you overcame, then use that experience and the lessons you gained from it to encourage and help you in your present circumstances.

Look deep and find the brave warrior that lies within. Do not accept defeat, you have the power, courage and strength to get through this situation that you are in!

Look in the mirror and see yourself with a vision of love and acceptance. Affirm to yourself your strengths, abilities and skills. By doing this, you will hold space to receive more abundance and love into your life.

The light inside you shines brighter than the darkness around you never forget that!

Success

This page is a sign that magnified abundance and success is on its way. All roads that lead to success require self-belief and hard work, but we want you to balance this by taking time out for yourself too.

Know that behind every successful person there have been many challenges, mistakes and failures. Be kind to yourself and know that all of these serve a purpose, even though it may not feel like it at the time.

Be aware of unexpected openings and opportunities that are offered to you. Do not let them pass you by because of fear or anxiety. Dissolve your fears by creating an image of a butterfly in your mind, blow it into your hand and then release your worries or uncertainties by blowing it out with love and light and visualising them fluttering away!

Let your imagination and creativity lead you to the fortune and dreams that you crave. It is then that your hard work and dedication will pay off and you will reap the rewards of the seeds that you have sown.

Balancing Relationships

We have been watching you and see that there is a deep need for you to balance your desires, goals and dreams with the relationships you have with others.

The labour of work, or what you are currently doing at present, requires a balance of commitment with your relationships with your loved ones. This is the driving force that enables you to succeed in any environment. Love is the pivotal force that catapults you to your destination! If what you are doing is burning you out, spend more time doing things that light you up! This will propel you further in the long-term.

Perhaps consider whether you are committed and working to the best of your ability in what you are doing and in your relationships with others. Are you being present in your relationships or are you too busy working, over-thinking or being consumed by technology?

If you become less distracted by things that are not beneficial to your soul, you will generate more time to invest in the things that you love the most. When you become more present, love, happiness and abundance will certainly arise.

Perseverance

No matter how hard the road ahead may seem, you must keep moving forward. Remember that forward is forward, however slow you go!

We are cheering you on, so keep pushing yourself in the direction of your purpose and soul calling! Believe in yourself and push through the limits that you or others place in your way. Tough situations build strong people!

Do not give up, even when you feel like you want to. The world loves a stubborn heart. If you fall or make mistakes, it is okay, you can still get back up! We believe in you.

Never think that you are a failure. You only fail when you stop trying! We are ushering, nudging and shaking you to move forward and keep going! You can do this!

If things are really draining your energy, take a break to relax and re-energise and then get back on the path you were walking. You may not have reached your destination just yet, but you are closer than you were yesterday.

Remember to be kind to yourself and do not be disheartened. It is often the last key in the bunch that opens the door to where you want to enter!

Moving others

We have seen that you have an inert ability to move people with either your presence, words or touch. You have a magnetic energy that attracts people into your field. Your power to inspire and empower others is moving, motivational and inspiring!

This ability you have to help others also creates a positive energy around you and sends ripples far and wide. You do not always see or hear about how you have impacted others, but we watch and see the beautiful ripples you have created. We want you to stop for a moment and acknowledge all that you are and all that you have done! For this we honour your soul and thank you!

It fills our hearts with joy to know that you can show people how to embrace what they perceive to be *'flaws'* or *'weaknesses'*. Know that the guidance you provide to other people helps them more than you realise, so continue to do what you are doing.

If new people cross your path or old people appear in your life, know that it is for a great purpose. Keep moving with the rhythm of your soul and it will guide you to where it yearns to go. There you will find satisfaction, joy, peace and love.

Self-Respect

We have seen that small pieces of you have been chipped away by people and circumstances. But it is time to re-inject yourself with confidence and re-empower yourself with self-respect!

Walk away or distance yourself from anyone who makes you feel less than you are worth or drains you of your dignity and self-respect. Remember that your value does *not* decrease based on someone's inability to see your worth!

Always speak from your authentic, loving self. Do not get drawn into any unnecessary dramas. Sometimes, the most powerful thing you can say and do is nothing! Do not allow your loyalty to become slavery. You do not owe anybody anything!

Save your help and guidance for someone who *does* deserve it. Those who value your support and treats you with the love and respect you so dearly deserve.

Your self-respect is sacred and one of your most treasured possessions. Remember who you are, reclaim your power back and learn to recognise when and what to let go of with love and light.

Faith in Yourself

See your current situation as a challenge and not as an obstacle. Trust in us and know that a positive outcome is being brought to you. It will align in your favour when the time is right. For now, continue moving forward with faith and remain patient and optimistic.

Know that faith can move mountains but remember, your doubts can create them. If you have lost someone dear to you, know that their presence in your life has given you the tools for you to move forward in difficult times. Reflect upon these and use them to help aid you at this crossroad. Only you can shift the course of your journey through the passage of your actions!

We encourage you to have faith in yourself. Do not ever give up because of one bad chapter in your life. Keep going and do not lose hope. Know that your story does not stop here. Miracles happen just before you are ready to quit!

Be mindful not to compare yourself to others. Learn to feel genuinely happy and content with who you are. Only you can decide who you want to be or what you want to do with the power of your mind and the faith you have in yourself.

We want you to know that you are amazing and you are good enough! Believe in yourself, as we believe in you!

Dreams

We want you to know that your dreams are important. So why put other people's dreams above your own? We want you to know that you matter! Anything is possible and everything is within reach if you have faith and believe in yourself.

Spending time focusing on things that do not serve you such as fear or judgements, will inevitably push your dreams further away from you. Creating a plan and then implementing it is a beneficial tool to help execute your dreams into your reality. Why allow your fears to erase or alter those dreams? The choice is yours!

Spend more time doing things or connecting with people that bring joy into your life. This will elevate you to new horizons. You have an abundance of love within you waiting to be unleashed, but only you can lower those barricades for it to fully shine and bask in it's ambience!

Pay attention to signs and messages that we send you. If you see peacocks, know that we are watching your progress and are proud of how strong and far you have come.

The impossible can come true. Do not let anyone stop you, but most importantly, do not be your own obstacle in reaching your dreams! You are an important part of the jigsaw, do not lose your place to anything or anyone! Make a move, there is no time like the present!

Love & Commitment

Self-love is an ocean and your heart is a vessel. Commitment into self-care will produce an over pour of love both for yourself and humanity!

This is a divine time to concentrate and put the love and commitment into what sets your soul on fire! The things that bring you joy make you happy, and when you are happy, abundance follows! You can then inject this into your work, relationships, goals or dreams.

Aim to keep your intentions and actions balanced and in unity. Take more time to balance your work, family and social life. When you have balance, everything else will begin to fall into place. If you act with love, you will receive acts of love in return.

Love is patient; quality time needs to be invested in yourself so that you can function better. If you decide to commit to something, make sure you invest the right amount of time and effort to fulfil this. Remember, love and commitment are acts not words.

Stay motivated and continuously remind yourself that YOU have the power to create the life you want, but you must invest in yourself with happiness and love first!

Disconnect To Reconnect

We want you to be mindful of your current environment. Know that you can walk away from anything that does not serve you or make you happy. This does not always mean just physically walking away, but mentally and emotionally too.

Declutter and disconnect from any negative words or actions, being mindful not to respond, react or retaliate. In these situations, silence is the best remedy. Do not be the one that fuels the fire, as the only person who will get burnt is you. Hold your integrity this is everything!

Have faith that any struggles you are facing at present will soon resolve. Spending time by yourself, reconnecting with mother nature, crystals or listening to meditation music will help you zone out from everything that distracts you. This will also help re-energise you and give you the nudge you need.

To hear yourself and our guidance, you need to be able to disconnect to reconnect again. This can only be done if you unplug the undesirable thoughts and people that pollute your mind! When you feel more grounded you can re-plug yourself into the world because you have rebooted your system to full optimism!

Faith

We surround and comfort you with a blanket of love and strength. Hold onto it tight and feel secure in the presence of our unconditional love. Faith is invisible, but it has the power to connect you to what you need.

Allow your faith and love to be bigger and stronger than your fears. Fear is an energy that contracts and love is an energy that expands. Envision a bright, white light encompassing your being whenever you feel deflated or like you want to give up. Love is light and this is what will help you expand!

Your faith can shift any obstacles but be mindful that your fears can also generate them. Let go of anything that weighs you down and do not doubt yourself! If doubt creeps in, inhale confidence and exhale fear.

You can change the scene of your life at any time from the energy around you. Spend time reconnecting with us and nature, drawing these harmonious energies into your soul.

Know that faith resides within your heart and it will give you the strength you need to take that next step. Have faith in yourself and trust that you have the power to overcome and do anything! If you see 222 or 2222, that is a direct message of guidance from us to remind you to *"Keep the Faith!"*

Actions

Your soul craves to joyfully serve humanity, but you need to be in an ocean of serenity and bliss to be able to swim and reach your destination.

The secret to success is when you put your mind, body, heart and soul into what you do with love and passion.

It is your love and passion that really fuels your actions in the right direction, which will bring about the change that is needed. To change and move forward, you must start with acting on your own needs first!

Once you have invested in yourself, think about your individual goals and reflect upon what needs to be done to acquire them. Put your energy and focus wholeheartedly into what it is you want to achieve.

Know that your actions mould you into who you want to become, but your words only say who you want to be! Remember that your actions speak louder than your words.

Plant the seeds you want and then plan on undertaking what it is you want to accomplish. Keep those thoughts aligned with only positive thoughts to yield more abundance.

Change Your Thoughts

Your life is a mere reflection of what you think. If you change your thoughts, you change your life. Work to balance the union of your mind with faith.

The joy that can enter your life is limitless. Joy, love, happiness and abundance is dependent upon the quality of your thoughts.

The more grateful you are for what you have, the better you will feel and the quicker your manifestations will appear.

Balance your thoughts with positivity and then tip the scales so your mindset is elevated above the negative events and people that infiltrate your life.

Let positivity dominate and take the central stage in your mind. It is time to serve an eviction notice to the negative committee that resides in your mind and get positive tenants to thrive inside! A happy mind is a happy home!

Invest in Yourself

We want to support you in fulfilling your potential. Spending time worrying about who likes or dislikes you will potentially deter you from your purpose. When you invest in your own thoughts, happiness will follow.

Life is a journey of ups and downs but you hold the key to create the life you desire. Happiness, love, success and dreams are all yours for the taking, but you must use the key to unlock those treasures. The key to doing this will be released when you learn to make yourself a priority. Self- love and care are imperative in the journey you embark upon. Self-love is not a selfish act but a necessary one!

Invest in filling yourself up with self-love and care because your life purpose is much greater than you know. You need to be optimising at full capacity to achieve all it is you intend on accomplishing. Listen to the whispers of what your body, heart, mind and soul need and then act upon them.

Invest your time, passion and commitment to your visions and goals and you will soon reap the rewards. The amount of energy you put in is what you will receive, but do not forget the greatest investment to propel forward is in yourself!

Joy

We love you for who you are and we want to see you filled with joy. We need you to accept yourself for the wonderful person you are and not be ashamed of how others see you.

If you are spending too much time attempting to make others happy, you are only sacrificing your own happiness in the process. Remember that you are only able to give to others that which you have yourself.

If you are not happy, self-care and maintenance need attending to. Always take the time to improve yourself before you start improving other people or things.

Remember that it is important to continuously bring joy into your life and to value yourself. When you are centred in joy, you have the power you need to swiftly move forward. If you are feeling trapped, give your worries to us and we will lift you up.

The key to being happy is knowing that you possess the power to choose what to accept and what to release. Let go of anything that does not serve you because it does not deserve you!

Inner Child

It is time to awaken and reconnect with your inner child again. This is where your true authentic self resides. It is the original piece of you that is pure, innocent and connected to your heart. Honour your inner child by living in the present moment of now. When you lose yourself in simple pleasures, you recognise how much there is to love about life.

This is how young children live and they are the most precious gifts in the world. It is now time to unleash your inner child as it wants to come out and play!

Spend time in the company of young children and observe their world through their eyes. Ask questions, get involved and perhaps you will see and feel the magic in everything too!

You may be growing on your journey and in age, but you can still stay young at heart if you unleash your inner child.

Remember when you were young, wild, curious and full of life and energy. Do not let life tame that beautiful authentic side. Embrace your inner child and you will experience a tremendous amount of love and healing. This is needed for your soul to thrive!

Ending of a Situation

You received this message because we want you to know that the ending of a situation and a beginning of a new one is near.

Remember that the relationships around you play an important part in your journey and all serve a purpose. Know that people come and go in your life like the seasons that constantly change. This can bring both pain and joy, but know that it will help both you and them in your growth and progression.

Be aware that it can be difficult to start the next chapter and end any situation you are in if you keep re-reading the last one. Release what is not serving you with love and light, so you can finish what was started, be that in work or a relationship.

Protect your energy and do not allow any negativity or drama to lower your vibration. Instead, turn this negative energy into fuel to succeed in any projects, ideas or work that you are currently undertaking. This is how you can turn pain into power!

When you make any decisions, have faith in the choices you make. Execute this with assertiveness, not allowing other people to doubt your choice. You know what benefits you. Trust your own authority and intuition for it will guide you well.

Overcoming Challenges

Rather than looking at problems as obstacles, see them as challenges that you can overcome. Unfortunately, being challenged in life is inevitable, but succumbing to it is optional. You have the choice to bulldoze through any challenges that you meet.

We understand that life can often feel difficult with these challenges that you face but have faith that you will reap the rewards if you continue to persevere and overcome your trials and tribulations.

Know that you have the strength that is needed to overcome every hurdle and adversity that you face. When you challenge yourself, you will realise the true potential of who you can become or what you can do!

Visualise yourself as a tree, keeping your roots grounded and you will be able to weather any storm. Remember that after every storm follows a rainbow!

Stand strong and have courage as your companion to guide your way. Keep the faith and know that the situation you are in will soon subside. We are working behind the scenes to help you. Trust in us as we trust in you!

Unison

When you are feeling downhearted or confused, it could be because your heart and mind are not working in harmony. Unity is strength and when the heart and mind work in unison, wonderful things can be achieved. Your body and soul will then gravitate towards love and joy.

In order to form in unison, fill your mind with gratitude and joyful memories that make you laugh or smile. Go for walks and breathe in the fresh air to rejuvenate your weary soul. When you are feeling lost, connecting and spending time in nature will help you find yourself again.

A lot has changed and will continue to change around you, and because of this, so will you! You are ready to come out of the cocoon that you are currently hibernating in so you can transform into a stronger and wiser being.

Cherish and appreciate what you have at present and what you have received. If you have lost something, think about the experiences, lessons and wisdom it brought you. It is when you choose to focus on the good things you have in your life rather than the things you do not have, that you begin to work in unison with your heart, body, mind and soul.

Divine Connection

You opened this page because we want you to know that everything you need is available to you when you connect with us. We want to get our messages through to you, but we cannot do this when you are not paying attention.

Communication is a two-way process and we want to talk to you! Take time to pray and meditate so that you can hear and feel our loving presence, support and guidance. We send you signs and synchronicities daily, but you need to slow down or stop to notice them!

Try to separate yourself from technology and the pressures and worries of life, in order to reconnect with us. Ensure that you reconnect with yourself too, by maintaining your needs and filling yourself up with self-love and care.

When you do this, you become more in-tune and in alignment with your being and soul's guidance. Only then will we be able to guide you at a much deeper level than we already are. Trust in us as we trust in you!

When you are connected to us, you become attuned to the solutions that you are seeking. This divine connection is a special avenue that will bring you transformation faster than you can imagine!

Growth

You have grown so much on this journey and we are proud of all you have done and achieved. Think of all the things you have achieved and what you are grateful for because these have contributed to your journey and where you are now.

You have an inert ability to shine your light but remember to make sure you protect your light so that you are not depleted. You cannot give to others if you do not have enough light to walk your own path.

You are the torch of divine love and light and we intend for you to share it with others, but do not give away your health in the process! It is okay to say, *"this isn't serving me"* and walk away in peace. You have the power to do this because you are a strong individual!

Remember that growth can be painful and lonely but like the caterpillar in the cocoon, with time and patience, you will break out of where you are residing and transform much stronger and more beautifully than before.

We would love to see you disengage from technology and reconnect with us and yourself. This is where you will grow in reflection.

Comfort

Even though you have walked through the darkest moments, we have always been present on your journey. We always embrace you with extra love and light to comfort you in such moments.

You may or may not have felt us but know that you have never been alone. We have been watching over you and we are proud of how far you have come, but we want you to be gentle on yourself.

Do not push yourself too much or kick yourself when you think you have made a *'mistake'*. That is how you grow and evolve. Know that it is okay to have bad days, or days when you want to scream and shout. If the only thing you have done all day is breathe, that is enough. Out of the suffering, hardships and traumas, we have seen your beautiful soul emerge and rise, time and time again. The warrior spirit within you can withstand any storm!

When your words fail you or you do not know what to say, know that silence carries the thoughts and prayers to your loved ones in your life and those who have transitioned. Your heart and soul will soon find comfort and peace. Have patience and trust in us. We send you an abundance of love and light to heal your heart.

We place an angelic kiss on your forehead. Feel the love, absorb it and use it to help you get through the next chapter of your journey. You are not alone!

Luck

We bring you good news… Your luck is about to change and abundance is on its way!

Keep your thoughts beating in tune with the rhythm of your heart and the sound of your dreams. However, be mindful that if your thoughts come out of alignment, everything on the outside can change too. Remain positive and open to the doors of opportunities that reveal themselves to you and walk through them with confidence.

Be conscious of how you use and nurture the lucky streak or abundance you receive. Think before you make any rash moves and this will inevitably support you in the long-term.

Recognise that faith, belief and perseverance assist you in acquiring the abundance that you receive. Do not forget to reward yourself for all your hard work too and show gratitude for the positive luck that you have received!

Relationship Cycles

We have noticed that you have been in the presence of people that are toxic, unsupportive or discouraging. We reach out to you to break out of these repetitive cycles. If you have done so already, we salute you for your courage, for we know how difficult it can be to detach from those you love or care for.

Understand that change occurs for a reason, as will the circle of friendships and relationships you are in. Allowing the fear to enter your space can delay or obstruct the changes and growth that is required for you to move forward.

We want you to know that we are here to lighten the load of what weighs you down by giving you the strength you need to rise above it. Change has a much grander purpose, which will serve you in the future.

Call upon us when fear creeps in. Equip yourself with your armour of courage and stand tall with conviction! You have a choice to walk away from any situation that does not feel right.

This is a good time to spend time with people who raise you up, not pull you down!

Synchronicity

You chose this page because we have been trying to get your attention. What you or others may deem a *"coincidence"* is in fact synchronicity. We are orchestrating and weaving a web for you to notice the patterns, signs and messages that stir the soul. This is us communicating to you!

We leave you a list of several ways we try to get through to you:

On your social media timeline and feeds, number sequences, feathers, rainbows, spirals, coins, sparks or animals.
Conversations with others or when reading, watching, listening to the tv, radio, books, magazines, newspapers, advertisements or internet.
In the clouds, epiphanies, visions, road signs.
In the music lyrics you hear or sounds, smells, feelings and senses that resonate or speak to you.

All of these signs above that you see or hear repetitively are prompting you to be aware of your thoughts, feelings and intentions. If you see one of these frequently, how does it make you feel? What does it represent to you? If you don't know, stop and think about it until something resonates!

It is time to wake up and notice the signs and messages we bless you with!

Take Small Steps

There is no need for you to rush into things. Instead, proceed forward with small steps first and take your time in making decisions with a clear, calm mind.

Make a conscious effort to think before you speak. Try to gather your thoughts and feelings first to prevent any explosive situations from occurring.

Relax, release and recharge when you need to. Life is all about progression and growth, but you are also here to experience happiness, satisfaction, and love. There is no need to put unnecessary pressure on yourself to move at a quicker pace.

We want you to know that there is no elevator to success. You must take one step at a time on your journey. Although the staircase may take longer, the rewards will be much more fulfilling at the end!

Progress is impossible without change, so take a chance on doing new things and more opportunities will appear. Remember that slow progress is better than no progress! Work hard but do not forget to play and enjoy yourself too.

Trust the Journey

You have awakened to the world around you and are beginning to understand the true mechanisms of how it works.

Continue to travel down the road of spiritual awakening and you will start to see and feel the light more than ever. When you trust the process of your journey, you will see everything unfold to ease you on your path.

Know that you can do anything you want and manifest anything you focus on. Relationships, financial and work goals will begin to manifest into form when you balance your spiritual and materialistic lifestyle. Give gratitude daily and soak yourself in self-love to recharge your energies, especially when you feel lost, down or drained. It is imperative to give your body what it needs!

You have overcome so much and because of that, you have the strength and power to get through anything that attempts to knock you down! You are a warrior and are protected by us.

Your Path

You have the power to do what you want! If you want to fly, clear your mind by releasing anything negative or toxic that does not serve you and weighs your beautiful wings down. You were born to fly on this path, not to be dragged down by other people!

Focus on what it is that YOU desire because you have independence in your own wings to take flight to where you choose to go. Remember that your thoughts influence the time it takes for you to get to your destination. Be aware that other people's thoughts, opinions and advice are only an offering. You can absorb what is useful and discard the rest with love and gratitude. You make the ultimate decisions along the path that you travel.

You are the author of your own story. You have the choice to write it the way you want it to go, whilst staying in control and not allowing anyone to influence the way it ends. That is your choice!

The pen you hold to write your story should remain in your hand. Be careful of '*who*' and '*what*' you share with others. If you give your pen away to others, they could potentially be writing your story for you!

Lightworker

You are a lightworker and here for a greater purpose. We are aware that you are at your happiest when you are helping others.

People are drawn to your veracious energy and the light that you radiate. Be aware of your own energy supply and ensure you are not depleting when offering help and advice to those who need it. With your highly attuned empathic abilities, it is quite easy to absorb their emotions or negativity to drain your own energy. It is vital that you learn to ground and protect your auric field!

In order to help make the world a better place and awaken others to the true beauty of life, it is essential to lead the way by example. Listen to your body and soul when you are feeling tired or low, this is a sign that your energy is depleted.

It is necessary to take time to rest and recharge your batteries and close yourself off temporarily for spiritual maintenance. You can only give and serve others if you are in a place where your own cup is overflowing.

Pay attention when you see lights flickering. This is a sign that we are with you and a reminder that you are guided and protected by the light. Your energy is a beautiful and powerful force. You have the power and gifts to raise the collective consciousness and shift humanity to another dimension!

Take Small Steps

There is no need for you to rush into things. Instead, proceed forward with small steps first and take your time in making decisions with a clear, calm mind.

Make a conscious effort to think before you speak. Try to gather your thoughts and feelings first to prevent any explosive situations from occurring.

Relax, release and recharge when you need to. Life is all about progression and growth, but you are also here to experience happiness, satisfaction, and love. There is no need to put unnecessary pressure on yourself to move at a quicker pace.

We want you to know that there is no elevator to success. You must take one step at a time on your journey. Although the staircase may take longer, the rewards will be much more fulfilling at the end!

Progress is impossible without change, so take a chance on doing new things and more opportunities will appear. Remember that slow progress is better than no progress! Work hard but do not forget to play and enjoy yourself too.

New Project

We want you to know that this is your life to live the way you want. You are in control of your own destiny!

If there is a new project you want to start or continue and you are feeling blocked or demotivated, take a step back to reflect. Consider what you feel is preventing you from growing and what you need to do to move forward. If it helps, write this down on a piece of paper so that you can see a clear structure on how to start or progress.

Focus on the end goal you wish to actualise and hold this clearly in your mind. Let go of any worries or concerns about how you are going to get there and trust that everything will work out.

No matter what your current circumstance is, if you are able to imagine something that sparks a light within your soul, you will be able to create something better for yourself.

Embrace your individuality within this new project and you will succeed in anything you do. There is no one else in the world like you and that is your unique power! Do not follow other people's footprints or path. Instead, create your own.

Self-Maintenance

It is easy to get wrapped up in the hustle and bustle of life, but it is important that you remember to take the time to stop and care for your mental, spiritual and physical wellbeing.

Make a conscious effort to introduce small habitual changes, focusing on self-maintenance. Give yourself time to relax, rest, take a break or have fun to enable your body to flow in its natural rhythmic state.

Indulge in things that make you feel good and increase your energy. When your mind, body and soul are nurtured, those things that cause you stress or worry are less likely to penetrate your energetic field.

Fill yourself up with self-love and care. Self-maintenance will help you re-energise and aid any healing that is needed.

When you give love and light to yourself, it will come back to you like a boomerang in other areas of your life. Love is the most powerful energy that can propel you forward and heal anything!

Reward Yourself

Yes, a big angelic high five from us! You have been working hard in all that you do and we want you to relax, unwind and reward yourself!

Give yourself credit for the good choices you have made or the things that you have been doing, however insignificant or small you may think it is. Remember that every action creates a ripple effect far and wide. We have seen these ripples and we are proud of the positive impact that you have had on those around you.

Know that it is okay to celebrate personal achievements, even if it is just getting out of bed in the morning or going to work when you do not want to. No one else may understand what it took for you to accomplish them but know your worth and reward yourself for anything good you have done.

You deserve to reward yourself and a little extra self-love and care will only fuel you further!

Synchronicity

You chose this page because we have been trying to get your attention. What you or others may deem a *"coincidence"* is in fact synchronicity. We are orchestrating and weaving a web for you to notice the patterns, signs and messages that stir the soul. This is us communicating to you!

We leave you a list of several ways we try to get through to you:

On your social media timeline and feeds, number sequences, feathers, rainbows, spirals, coins, sparks or animals.
Conversations with others or when reading, watching, listening to the tv, radio, books, magazines, newspapers, advertisements or internet.
In the clouds, epiphanies, visions, road signs.
In the music lyrics you hear or sounds, smells, feelings and senses that resonate or speak to you.

All of these signs above that you see or hear repetitively are prompting you to be aware of your thoughts, feelings and intentions. If you see one of these frequently, how does it make you feel? What does it represent to you? If you don't know, stop and think about it until something resonates!

It is time to wake up and notice the signs and messages we bless you with!

You Can Do It!

We want you to know that you can do anything when you put your mind, body, heart and soul into it. You are a powerful being of love and light. Lead your life as a positive example to others. If you fall, get back up! You are a warrior!

People around you may criticise or doubt what you say or do, but you can use this as fuel to propel you forward and show them what you are really made of!

Know that you CAN do anything. Anything is possible if you conceive it in your mind first! If you are offered support from people around you, do not be proud or dismiss them. You have the choice to let go of pride, anger or resentment and accept the help that is offered to you if it resonates. This is us supporting and guiding you in your times of need, orchestrating the people to be in the right place at the right time for you.

If there is a new job, project or idea that you feel passionate about, put those thoughts into action. If you have already started something and have not finished it, get it back out and start *operation revival!*

Actions are what get the ball rolling. Nothing will move or change otherwise!

Release

We have noticed that you have been holding onto things, which are suppressing your true authentic self. You must heal and restore yourself by releasing any fears or emotions that are blocking you. Resisting this process will only deter you from your path. You have the strength to face anything!

You may feel that a lot of issues you face run in your family, but we are here to guide, empower and reassure you that this pattern does not need to continue with you. You can break the ancestral ties that are preventing you from moving forward.

Know that you can transform pain into power and even empower others from your own personal experiences. This includes any trials, tribulations or harrowing events you have faced.

When you choose not to respond to an emotional impulse such as anger, rage or heartache, you are halfway there! Release any emotional energy and focus on acceptance, as this will help restore the balance.

Know that the past can be painful, but the beautiful thing about it is that it forces you to learn what does not serve or benefit you for your present and future journeys.

Warrior Spirit

It takes great force to face other people's opinions and criticisms, but you can overcome this. We know that you have done it before and we want you to know that you can do it again! When you can silence other people's voices from your mind, your own voice can prevail!

This is your life and nobody else's, so take the reins and control it by releasing the warrior spirit within you! Be courageous and assertive in any decisions that you make. Rather than thinking about what you cannot do, focus your thoughts and attention on what you can and will do!

You are standing with an army of Angels beside you, you can do anything! There is no need to lower your expectations to fit in. You are perfect just as you are! We want you to know that you were born to shine, so never let anyone dim your beautiful sparkle.

Everything you need is already inside you! That is the secret people do not tell you. When you feel like giving up, we are the voice of hope that whispers, *"try again!"*

Your warrior spirit will always succeed because you were born with it!

Self-Respect

We have seen that small pieces of you have been chipped away by people and circumstances. But it is time to re-inject yourself with confidence and re-empower yourself with self-respect!

Walk away or distance yourself from anyone who makes you feel less than you are worth or drains you of your dignity and self-respect. Remember that your value does *not* decrease based on someone's inability to see your worth!

Always speak from your authentic, loving self. Do not get drawn into any unnecessary dramas. Sometimes, the most powerful thing you can say and do is nothing! Do not allow your loyalty to become slavery. You do not owe anybody anything!

Save your help and guidance for someone who *does* deserve it. Those who value your support and treats you with the love and respect you so dearly deserve.

Your self-respect is sacred and one of your most treasured possessions. Remember who you are, reclaim your power back and learn to recognise when and what to let go of with love and light.

Divine Connection

You opened this page because we want you to know that everything you need is available to you when you connect with us. We want to get our messages through to you, but we cannot do this when you are not paying attention.

Communication is a two-way process and we want to talk to you! Take time to pray and meditate so that you can hear and feel our loving presence, support and guidance. We send you signs and synchronicities daily, but you need to slow down or stop to notice them!

Try to separate yourself from technology and the pressures and worries of life, in order to reconnect with us. Ensure that you reconnect with yourself too, by maintaining your needs and filling yourself up with self-love and care.

When you do this, you become more in-tune and in alignment with your being and soul's guidance. Only then will we be able to guide you at a much deeper level than we already are. Trust in us as we trust in you!

When you are connected to us, you become attuned to the solutions that you are seeking. This divine connection is a special avenue that will bring you transformation faster than you can imagine!

Trust the Journey

You have awakened to the world around you and are beginning to understand the true mechanisms of how it works.

Continue to travel down the road of spiritual awakening and you will start to see and feel the light more than ever. When you trust the process of your journey, you will see everything unfold to ease you on your path.

Know that you can do anything you want and manifest anything you focus on. Relationships, financial and work goals will begin to manifest into form when you balance your spiritual and materialistic lifestyle. Give gratitude daily and soak yourself in self-love to recharge your energies, especially when you feel lost, down or drained. It is imperative to give your body what it needs!

You have overcome so much and because of that, you have the strength and power to get through anything that attempts to knock you down! You are a warrior and are protected by us.

Courage

We are here to give you the strength and courage you need so you do not resist the changes that are unravelling in your life. These changes are here to help you evolve and grow, not to create a feeling of being stuck or paralysed. Gather and receive the strength that we send you and stand tall to whatever comes your way.

Have the courage to make the changes you need and the strength to see them through. You can do this! You are strong! Even though it may feel like everything around you could be falling apart, perhaps it is really falling into place. We see this and in time you will too.

It takes great strength to stand alone! We admire and love this quality you possess. Your individuality brings you the gift of freedom and flight. It takes great courage to become who you are, and for this you will be rewarded with great abundance.

Remember to maintain the connection with yourself by staying in the present moment of now. Remain balanced, grounded and aware so that you have the clarity to summon the power of strength and courage that dwells within your beautiful soul.

You have a warrior spirit. Do not allow your past to define you.

Your past does not define your destiny!

Dreams

We want you to know that your dreams are important. So why put other people's dreams above your own? We want you to know that you matter! Anything is possible and everything is within reach if you have faith and believe in yourself.

Spending time focusing on things that do not serve you such as fear or judgements, will inevitably push your dreams further away from you. Creating a plan and then implementing it is a beneficial tool to help execute your dreams into your reality. Why allow your fears to erase or alter those dreams? The choice is yours!

Spend more time doing things or connecting with people that bring joy into your life. This will elevate you to new horizons. You have an abundance of love within you waiting to be unleashed, but only you can lower those barricades for it to fully shine and bask in it's ambience!

Pay attention to signs and messages that we send you. If you see peacocks, know that we are watching your progress and are proud of how strong and far you have come.

The impossible can come true. Do not let anyone stop you, but most importantly, do not be your own obstacle in reaching your dreams! You are an important part of the jigsaw, do not lose your place to anything or anyone! Make a move, there is no time like the present!

Your Path

You have the power to do what you want! If you want to fly, clear your mind by releasing anything negative or toxic that does not serve you and weighs your beautiful wings down. You were born to fly on this path, not to be dragged down by other people!

Focus on what it is that YOU desire because you have independence in your own wings to take flight to where you choose to go. Remember that your thoughts influence the time it takes for you to get to your destination. Be aware that other people's thoughts, opinions and advice are only an offering. You can absorb what is useful and discard the rest with love and gratitude. You make the ultimate decisions along the path that you travel.

You are the author of your own story. You have the choice to write it the way you want it to go, whilst staying in control and not allowing anyone to influence the way it ends. That is your choice!

The pen you hold to write your story should remain in your hand. Be careful of *'who'* and *'what'* you share with others. If you give your pen away to others, they could potentially be writing your story for you!

Balance

Although the road you travel upon may be difficult, unpleasant, challenging or testing, trust that you can overcome those feelings. Aim to balance your thoughts and feelings to maintain stability and equilibrium. For every bad thought or feeling, cancel it out with a good thought.

Know that your body is a temple, so keep it filled with love and good thoughts. This is a healthy habitat for your soul to live and flourish in. What benefits your soul benefits your life! The more you care for it, the more blessings and abundance you will receive.

Balance is about two things: h*olding on* versus l*etting go.*

Hold onto memories and experiences that lift your soul and make you smile.

If something is no longer positively affecting your life, would it benefit you to let it go? If you do not let go of what is not serving you, will you be able to receive what you truly deserve? With the knowledge that everything you need is on the other side of fear, would you jump?

Taking that leap of faith could benefit you, but only if you balance your thoughts enough to tip the scale and have the confidence to jump!

Comfort

Even though you have walked through the darkest moments, we have always been present on your journey. We always embrace you with extra love and light to comfort you in such moments.

You may or may not have felt us but know that you have never been alone. We have been watching over you and we are proud of how far you have come, but we want you to be gentle on yourself.

Do not push yourself too much or kick yourself when you think you have made a 'mistake'. That is how you grow and evolve. Know that it is okay to have bad days, or days when you want to scream and shout. If the only thing you have done all day is breathe, that is enough. Out of the suffering, hardships and traumas, we have seen your beautiful soul emerge and rise, time and time again. The warrior spirit within you can withstand any storm!

When your words fail you or you do not know what to say, know that silence carries the thoughts and prayers to your loved ones in your life and those who have transitioned. Your heart and soul will soon find comfort and peace. Have patience and trust in us. We send you an abundance of love and light to heal your heart.

We place an angelic kiss on your forehead. Feel the love, absorb it and use it.

Unleashing Love

Love is the most powerful energy known to mankind and you hold the power to unleash it from within your beautiful being! We want you to know that it is not about changing yourself, it is about loving yourself. You do not need anyone else to complete who you are, you can do that yourself!

If you are in a situation that you have been in before and it is impinging on your heart, change needs to occur for you to progress. Reflect upon your past experiences with what is happening now. Notice the similarities and differences and then consider what you could do differently. If something keeps repeating, perhaps deeper lessons need to be learned to help with your spiritual growth.

Love requires hard work, time, commitment and passion.

If you feel like you have a hole in your heart, the only person that can fill and complete it is you!

We feel the pains contained within your heart as they are ours too. We know that your heart needs love, but the greatest gift you can give yourself is to spend more time on loving yourself! It is then that you can break free of any cycles or patterns that are holding you back. That is the magnificent ripple effect of unleashing self-love and care!

Motivation

A wealth of infinite abundance will be yours if you are motivated enough to attain it. The biggest source of motivation is in your thoughts. Train your mind to keep trying, not allowing thoughts of failure to tie you down.

Fearing failure can essentially cancel out your motivational streak. When you feed fear with more fear, it thrives on this environment to survive. Instead, have no limits and make no excuses, otherwise fear will continue to breed. You can do anything if you completely immerse your mind, body, heart and soul into it, with passion and love!

If you get knocked down, what motivates you to get back up?

Whatever this is, you can use it to push yourself every day because no one else is going to do it for you. This does not mean you need to overexert yourself. Small steps are okay too, there is no rush.

Spend time reflecting and planning what you need to do first and this will help you be more efficient and will save you time in the long run. The time and dedication you pour into what you are doing or intend to do, will produce an overpour of abundance.

So put your motivation pants on and get moving!

Energy & Vibration

You can create abundance with the power of your mind but be aware when your mind is acting like a yo-yo and your thoughts are up and down. This is a sign that you need to stop!

Allowing negative thoughts to dominate your mind will only attract negativity back towards you. Allowing anxiety, doubt, fear and worry to distract you, will lower your vibrations! Instead, focus your energy in being with people who you love and make you feel happy and content. Maintain this state of mind and you will open a gateway for abundance to flow through.

Put your time and energy into setting your intentions with belief and hope. Visualise what it is that you want. Feel it, believe it and imagine receiving it. The positive vibrations of energy that you emit, you will attract!

Once your mind is released from the prison of your thoughts, you will be more open to obtain what you desire because you are vibrating at a higher frequency. Your thoughts and words are a vibration of energy. You must learn to change them so you are vibrating on a harmonious frequency to support what it is you want to receive.

Remember, the raw capability of the mind is limitless!

Move with Love

Love is the driver that steers you towards your destination. You cannot move without it. It will benefit you if you let go of any resentment or anger you hold onto, because it will only prevent you from moving forward diligently.

If you feel like your emotions are taking control of you, spend time meditating or praying, clearing your mind from distractions so you can receive the guidance you need.

Make a conscious effort to spend more time with those you love and be grateful for what you have and how you received it. In order to build on your relationships, commitment is required by investing time and love into them. But first you need to pour love into yourself. This is not essential, it is necessary!

The source of your actions should always come from a place of love. Work hard on giving love daily to yourself then to those around you and the work you do.

Spend time doing something that satisfies your soul. Time invested in self-care and love will rejuvenate and re-energise you, so that you can focus on the outcome you want to receive.

Energy

We have noticed that your mind and body have been in constant over-drive. We suggest creating time to relax, take a break or slow down.

Take time to meditate or connect to our divine energy. You have the power to access it whenever you want and to gain a deeper insight. Tap into this energy as it will guide you on your journey.

Life is for enjoying and when you enjoy what you are doing, your energy naturally amplifies. You will then be vibrating on a higher frequency and become much more proficient in what you do.

The energy you emit creates your life. If you are feeling drained or tired, your energy is not functioning as well as it could be. Take some time to stop and recharge in order to heal your soul and receive the optimal energy for you to perform.

Keep your vibrations elevated by ensuring you are looking after your wellbeing. Fill yourself up with self-love, care and worth. This is a necessity for your journey!

High vibrational energy is infectious and has the aptitude to spread ripples far and wide. For what you deliver, you also receive!

Relationship Cycles

We have noticed that you have been in the presence of people that are toxic, unsupportive or discouraging. We reach out to you to break out of these repetitive cycles. If you have done so already, we salute you for your courage, for we know how difficult it can be to detach from those you love or care for.

Understand that change occurs for a reason, as will the circle of friendships and relationships you are in. Allowing the fear to enter your space can delay or obstruct the changes and growth that is required for you to move forward.

We want you to know that we are here to lighten the load of what weighs you down by giving you the strength you need to rise above it. Change has a much grander purpose, which will serve you in the future.

Call upon us when fear creeps in. Equip yourself with your armour of courage and stand tall with conviction! You have a choice to walk away from any situation that does not feel right.

This is a good time to spend time with people who raise you up, not pull you down!

Healing

Your health is of great importance to us and we want you to function in its full capacity. We love and care about you but we need you to do the same too!

Commit to yourself by maintaining your physical, emotional, psychological and spiritual needs. Eat foods that nourish your body and indulge in healthy habits.

Be present and surround yourself in high vibrational environments such as listening to uplifting, empowering music or affirming strong, inspiring, daily mantras to elevate your emotional and psychological state of mind.

Heal in the presence of nature; listen to uplifting or serene music, soak in a salt bath, exercise, treat yourself, practice daily gratitude, read self-help books, practice mindfulness, meditation, prayer, yoga and Pilates.

If you feel like you are overthinking and struggling to tame your thoughts, try taking time to practise any of the above. This will enable space for enriching things to attract to you. When you are at peace with yourself, happiness will follow and this will aid the healing process.

Patience

We can see your frustration in a specific area of your life and we want you to know we are supporting you. Trust in us and have patience.

Patience is not about the ability to wait, but the attitude you have whilst waiting! Build a relationship by communicating daily to your inner and outer needs and take the time to nurture them. You do not necessarily need a mind that is speaking, but a patient heart that is listening. It is then that the insight and support you require will be presented to you.

Learn to accept that things can happen in different ways, rather than the ways that you expect. Everything happens for a divine reason and everything is coming together as it should to benefit you in the best way possible.

Have faith that opportunities and abundance will soon be presented to you. Do not allow your faith to waiver. Worry and fear ends where faith begins. Remain patient and know that everything comes in divine timing. Trust in us.

The best things in life are worth waiting for!

Declutter

If you feel like your life is full of chaos and disharmony, this is a sign that you need to declutter!

Clutter is not just the things in your wardrobe or in the environment around you, it is anything that gets between you and the life that you want to be living. This includes the clutter that resides within your mind too!

Start decluttering your mind and the environment around you. If it does not nourish your soul, get rid of it. It is the unnecessary things that you hold onto that have the aptitude to stunt your growth. If your possessions or thoughts that you hold onto are not serving you, it will not be serving you any better in a box collecting dust or locked up in your mind. Releasing what does not serve you helps your mind and body heal on many levels.

Making space in both your environment and mind allows new opportunities, relationships and ideas to enter your field. When you release the baggage that holds you down, you feel lighter and begin to soar to new heights!

The *"Out with the old and in with the new"* motto springs to our mind! Perhaps you can use this as your affirmation to aid your task of decluttering!

Luck

We bring you good news… Your luck is about to change and abundance is on its way!

Keep your thoughts beating in tune with the rhythm of your heart and the sound of your dreams. However, be mindful that if your thoughts come out of alignment, everything on the outside can change too. Remain positive and open to the doors of opportunities that reveal themselves to you and walk through them with confidence.

Be conscious of how you use and nurture the lucky streak or abundance you receive. Think before you make any rash moves and this will inevitably support you in the long-term.

Recognise that faith, belief and perseverance assist you in acquiring the abundance that you receive. Do not forget to reward yourself for all your hard work too and show gratitude for the positive luck that you have received!

Cultivation

We want you to know that your body and mind needs to be cultivated in order to work effectively and efficiently. What you feed your body is just as important as what you feed your mind.

Fertilising your mind with kindness and love, and your body with healthy habits and substances, are vital! When they are both functioning in unison, this will produce a reservoir of energy.

If you have something to start or complete, now is the time to address it. Everything that you have been contemplating, planning or doing will start to come together when action is taken. Your hard work will inevitably pay off and you will start to reap the rewards, but you must have the energy contained within for you to release the energy needed to harvest your intended outcome.

The journey from the start of conception to completion may be challenging but enjoy and embrace every moment by remaining present. Having the determination and patience, whilst learning from the challenges you may face will be an asset to usher you along the way.

Take the necessary steps to start or complete what you set out to do by cultivating what you wish to grow. It is then that you will be rewarded with fruits from the seeds that you have planted!

Completion

You chose this page because we need to give you a gentle nudge in the right direction!

We are here to remind you to take the steps and actions required to continue moving forward or completing intended goals. Habit, persistence and perseverance is what will see you through to the end.

If you have an idea, start to implement it now, envisioning it in completeness. If you have already started something, continue to execute it to the finish line. Do not expect others to do it for you - the ball is in your court now! It takes focus, determination and practise to aim high in order to succeed.

Achievement, success, desire and dreams are all connected with action. Even if you feel like you will or are making *'mistakes'*, keep moving and do not give up. You can do anything if you shift your mind into positive gear! When you do, you will be cruising in the fast lane in no time!

The best thing you can invest in is YOU! Have faith and courage in your own abilities and see things through to the end.

Abundance

We want you to focus on what you have, rather than on what you do not have. Everything you need, you have access to! The wealth of abundance you obtain from within is priceless and extraordinarily limitless!

We know that the situation you have been facing comes from a deep-rooted perception of wealth that has been embedded within you, from a combination of other people, past lives and conditioning. We want to reassure you that money is not to be feared, nor is it the route of all evil! The fear of not having enough money is really an embedded fear that you are not enough. We want you to know that you are enough, and you are all that you need! When you begin to accept this, you will start to detangle and cut the cords of ancestral ties that bind you.

Remember, there is more to life than materialistic possessions.

It is better to be broke with a beautiful heart than rich with intentions that do not serve you! Do what sets your soul on fire by living in the present moment of 'Now' and you will attract all the love and abundance into your life that you require.

Take time each day to express what you are grateful for; from the love that you receive from others, to the air that you breathe that keeps you alive. When you practise this daily, abundance will shift in your favour!

Growth

You have grown so much on this journey and we are proud of all you have done and achieved. Think of all the things you have achieved and what you are grateful for because these have contributed to your journey and where you are now.

You have an inert ability to shine your light but remember to make sure you protect your light so that you are not depleted. You cannot give to others if you do not have enough light to walk your own path.

You are the torch of divine love and light and we intend for you to share it with others, but do not give away your health in the process! It is okay to say, *"this isn't serving me"* and walk away in peace. You have the power to do this because you are a strong individual!

Remember that growth can be painful and lonely but like the caterpillar in the cocoon, with time and patience, you will break out of where you are residing and transform much stronger and more beautifully than before.

We would love to see you disengage from technology and reconnect with us and yourself. This is where you will grow in reflection.

Self-Worth

Self-worth is vital for your wellbeing and happiness. If you do not feel good about yourself, how can you feel good about anything or anyone else?

Know your worth and do not settle for less than you deserve! Why allow people at work or in relationships to treat you inadequately, just because you love them or because of what they have done for you? Remember you do not owe anybody anything!

We want you to know that you do not need to find your self-worth in other people, you can only find it within yourself. It is then that you will be able to attract a job or relationship that is worthy of you! Work on being in love with the person that you see in the mirror, that person who has been through so much and is still standing!

Nobody is entitled to treat you less than your worth. If they do, learn to walk away or distance yourself from them because they will only continue holding you down and suppressing the beautiful being that you are.

Do not allow anyone to dull your beautiful sparkle, you were born to shine!

Compassion

We want you to know that every small act of kindness goes a long way. You are here to make an impact in the world but remember sometimes less is more!

Working hard and earning money is not the only way to success. Do not underestimate the power of a hug, smile, a kind word or compliment; a shoulder for someone to cry on or a listening ear. They can have the potential to turn someone's whole life around.

Compassion not only helps others rise but it also helps you too. If you want to be happy and turn your life around, try practising compassion with yourself too! Here is our extra nudge of guidance to you:

Consider reducing the food, people or environments that deplete your energy and leave you feeling tired, frustrated, or low.

Add some fun, adventure and happiness into your life as part of your daily routine.

Relax and rejuvenate your mind and body by disconnecting with technology for at least half an hour before going to bed.

Engage with us and connect with mother nature by getting some fresh air and re-connecting back to source.

Have compassion for yourself, by taking CARE of you!

Love

We want you to know that we love you, but we want you to love yourself too! When you feel love for yourself, that love will enable the strength and courage your warrior spirit has to transform pain into power!

Take time for self-care by doing something that you love and enjoy. Be mindful of what you say, think, feel, do and eat. They all require attention and awareness so you can flourish.

If something hurts, let it ricochet off you by responding with love. If you harness your emotions in the direction of love, you become more balanced.

If your thoughts and feelings are taking control of you, ground yourself. Inner peace is required in this situation. To find it, silence your mind from distractions. Do not be in a rush to do or say things.

Let any worries bounce off your energetic field and release yourself from the shackles of fear that burdens you. It is then that you will be able to drop the load that weighs you down, so that you can spread your wings and fly in the direction of what you love.

Journal

Journal

Journal

Journal

Journal

Journal

Journal

Journal

Journal

Journal

Journal

Journal

Journal

Journal

Journal

Journal

Journal

Journal

Journal

Journal

Journal

Journal

Journal

Journal

Journal

Journal

Journal

Journal

Journal

Journal

Journal

Journal

Journal

Printed in Great Britain
by Amazon

61668838R00214